What Gap?

[signature]

Jessie Gordon

A Communication Tool Box

What Gap?

Acknowledgements

The ideas my company EPT uses, many of which appear in this book, are inspired both consciously and sometimes unconsciously by numerous well-proven disciplines and techniques, including some used in the performing arts. Particular individuals have been pivotal in this process, for example Keith Yon (one of my most fascinating teachers at Dartington College of Arts), some of my friends and colleagues in the Pip Simmons Theatre Group, and dear friends and colleagues in EPT, most notably Jacqueline von Preuss (a founding member, who designed the original EPT voice work), Maggie Scott (in particular with her collaboration in the area of gender and cross cultural knowledge) and then Mary Lou Collins, Ian Kantor, Judith Herzberg, Roderic Leigh, Sandra in 't Veld and Henk van der Meulen, who have each at different times been an important sounding board and support. I have also been influenced and inspired by ancient techniques such as Tai Chi, as well as the work of more contemporary individuals, for example Moshe Feldenkrais.

Additional thanks to:
Henk, Max and Ruby for being a daily inspiration, Robert Glick for helping me get started with this book and Joost van den Ossenblok (A.W. Bruna publishers) for his valuable guidance and enthusiasm in getting this book published, Carel van Bemmelen, Ton Geurts and Mirella Visser for their encouraging feedback and support, Hester Lenstra, Bob George, Maarten van Vliet, Dick Bartelse along with Mary Lou Collins and Sandra in 't Veld for agreeing to read through an earlier script and give me the feedback I needed, Constance Kaine for taking the time and advising me, Gerda Kappelhof, Marty Cruikshank, Maggie Scott, Lorraine T. Miller, Krisna Lee Hanks, Lisa Ross, Laura Carmichael, Margot Nies, Adella Langdon, Claudia Trajano Faria, Claudia Kratzheller and Ard Nouwen for years of loyalty and EPT collaboration, Brigitte Dewasme and Jaco Groot for thinking along with me, Penelope Goodare for her sharp editing skills, Toni Mulder and Merel Meurs for their creative and strong design, the thousands of EPT programme participants who over the years have inspired the continuous development of these ideas and finally without which none of this could have happened – the many companies and individuals who have invested in booking the EPT programmes.

Defining the Words Leader & Leadership

The ideas in this communication tool box are particularly relevant for anyone who already is or aspires to be a leader.

Meaning: someone who guides decision-making processes with one or more people, which lead to action and change. And someone who takes responsibility for the consequences of guiding such actions, which will most often affect other people's lives.

It is a role of accountability.

This can take many forms:
→ Parents, teachers and professors who guide and lead the development of young people.
→ Business people who have managerial responsibilities.
→ Directors of a group, institution or company of any size.
→ Politicians or leaders of a political party or country.
→ Doctors or health workers who guide the health of patients.

When the words leader or leadership are used in this book they mean any of the above.

I acknowledge that there are certainly different layers and implications of responsibilities in any leadership position. A simple example is the difference between a decision or an action which affects one, several hundred, thousands or millions of people.

© Jessie Gordon, 2013
© A.W. Bruna Uitgevers B.V. Amsterdam
Design: Mulder van Meurs, Amsterdam
Cover photo: Merlijn Doomernik

ISBN   978 94 005 0301 4
NUR   770

Tweede druk, november 2014

For reasons of privacy certain names in this book have been changed.

All rights reserved. *Without limiting the rights under copyright reserved above, no part of this book may be reproduced, stored in or introduced into a retrieval system, or transmitted, in any form or by any means (electronic, mechanical, photocopying, recording or otherwise) without the written permission of both the copyright owner and the author of the book.*

for Beryl & Ruby

What Gap?
Why & How to Use this Book

Consider the idea that regular quality contact and mutual understanding are not only pleasant but almost as vital to our survival as food, sleep or oxygen. And this is why we respond so positively to anyone who has the skills to close the UNDERSTANDING GAP.

It is quality contact and mutual understanding which will enable us to not only survive but also thrive.

The question is: what are the essential building blocks needed to close the UNDERSTANDING GAP between what we think we are saying and how others actually perceive us?

This book is a communication tool box for people who wish to take the lead and make a difference. It identifies these building blocks and takes you along the path of successfully implementing them.

Two individuals communicate similar information in the context of a live interaction. One person is easily understood on a factual level, as well as stimulating collaborative, creative thinking. The other is hard to understand, uninspiring on an emotional level and tiring or even annoying to listen to. *"I don't know how I managed to stay awake..."* The second person created a large UNDERSTANDING GAP. And maybe did not even realise it...

If we occupy the same space as other people each of us will be continually receiving and sending out different messages, whether we intend to or not. In a live social context there is never a moment when we will be able to communicate *'nothing at all'*. This is regardless of whether we are speaking or silent. If we have the skills during live communications to close the UNDERSTANDING GAPs, our effect on everyone around us can be significant. Whether it is with our friends and family, or in the professional or political arena.

When given the choice we usually prefer to spend time with an individual or group who we understand and with whom we can easily communicate. We enjoy the click. Even more than just enjoying it, we are more likely to excel when we feel understood. Humans are not solitary animals; contact with each other is a basic drive. When put in solitary confinement, many people – depending on their character – will eventually descend into insanity. On a daily basis people regularly experience moments of isolation, in the form of either not understanding or not being understood by others. The negative feelings which this isolation so often elicits are *'maddening'*. In the English language we sometimes use the word mad: *"I was mad at them…" "It made me feel so mad…"* to replace the word angry. How often does the reaction to the frustration of not being understood, manifest itself in some form of anger or rage?

Often the deciding factor in choosing to be with or work with a person, a group of people or an organisation will be when trust is established through an inter-personal click. On a world stage with the ever-more globalised economies it is increasingly common to communicate within a mix of national differences; to be effective each one of us will need to increase communication sensitivity and flexibility to reduce or close the cultural divide.

Although our society regularly gives the credit for innovative ideas to individual people, once we look under the surface we see that human brilliance comes through a combination of accomplished leadership and team thinking. Winning collaborations are rooted in our ability to effectively understand and be inspired by each other. One of the biggest obstacles, which all too often gets in the way of closing these complex UNDERSTANDING GAPs, is ourselves. Not because we are being insensitive, but because most of us have probably never studied how to do this. The skills needed to make useful selections of incoming messaging and create clear strategic outgoing messaging, thus closing the complex UNDERSTANDING GAPs, are given very little attention during our upbringing and education.

And yet it is not random or mysterious.
I have been fascinated by this topic since childhood, and over many years of studying and working in experimental theatre, the visual arts and a twelve month stint in a rock band, I have absorbed and developed countless ideas on the subject of communication. As a co-founder, creator and director of Executive Performance Training (EPT) for more than twenty years, I have applied and refined them. To date, several thousand professionals have passed through our hands.

During the years I identified the building blocks needed to close the UNDERSTANDING GAP between the message we think we are putting across and the message others actually receive.

I have regularly been asked to document these ideas and experiences. The aim of this book is to give the tools and to take the ideas past just reading into experiencing behavioural change, in bite sized portions. The reader will not have to take *'time out'* but rather can see how to take *'time in'*, weaving the process and information into daily life. The quick fix-it of a sensational learning moment, although fun and attractive, all too often evaporates. With the danger of initially becoming overly aware, the intention of this book is to take you through a longer process of which PLEASURE is definitely a component. In certain situations ignorance may be bliss. If you feel that investigating the breadth and depth of communication may be an ignorance-is-bliss case for you... please go no further... stop reading!

Each section of the book is intended to be self-contained. You can either read it sequentially from beginning to end or dip randomly into the ideas that appeal to you, motivated by the section headings. Many of the ideas are interrelated, so there is a certain amount of cross-over. However, one of our learning mechanisms is through re-experiencing. With this book through the experiencing, experimenting and building up of the ideas from different angles you will increase your personal perception, understanding and communication potential.

To guide your choice the sections are divided into three clusters: **Golden Classics, Under the Skin** and **No Man's Land**. Try reading a section and then experimenting with those particular ideas for a week or so before moving on to the next. Become a private eye, investigating the daily moment-to-moment effectiveness of communication and leadership. Enjoy!

As the Irish playwright George Bernard Shaw noted,
'The single biggest problem in communication is the illusion that it has taken place.'

Contents

Golden Classics

23	1	Choice – Importance & Priority
31	2	Flexibility with Holding On & Letting Go
39	3	The Body – Physicality & Gesture
55	4	Space
69	5	Eyes & Contact
79	6	Our Voice
91	7	Tempo, Timing & Cross Cultural Understanding
101	8	Silence
109	9	Giving & Receiving
119	10	Levels of Listening – Distracted Versus Focussed
125	11	Crying in Public
135	12	The Power of Laughter
143	13	The Smile Confusion

Under the Skin

153	1	**Habits & Personal Rituals Are Not Who We Are**
161	2	**Identity**
173	3	**Authenticity – I/ME & US/WE**
183	4	**Negotiating Self-Worth**
195	5	**Meeting as Equals**
203	6	**Conscious of Self Versus Self-Conscious**
211	7	**Fearless or Fearful**
219	8	**When Taking Risks Is Motivating & Inspiring**
227	9	**Pleasure**
235	10	**Balance As a Verb**
241	11	**Wholes & Holes**

No Man's Land

251	**1**	**Past . Present . Future**
261	**2**	**Intuition & Gut (re-) Action**
269	**3**	**Non-Judgemental Perception & Positive Re-Enforcement Lead to Creativity**
281	**4**	**Right or Wrong ... Good or Bad**
291	**5**	**Trust & Belief**
303	**6**	**Embracing Ambiguity**
311	**7**	**Repetition – Does It Exist?**
319	**8**	**What & How Do Others Remember What You Have Said**
329	**9**	**Strategic Emotion**
341	**10**	**Distance & Intimacy**
351	**11**	**Inclusion & Exclusion**
365	**12**	**Diversity & Decision-Making**
375	**13**	**Leading & Following – A Brief Look**

Golden Classics

1 Choice
Importance & Priority

This section includes two AND-DO-ITs

...Mmmmmm the vodka tastes good, shall I have another sip...

Deciding what to do and when to do it is continual. As I write this I am being bombarded with different stimuli, which are asking for a decision: I am a bit hot, shall I take off my jumper? It is getting dark, shall I turn on another light? I am getting hungry, shall I go and eat now or later, shall I eat at home or go out to a restaurant? Do I want to finish this thought, shall I stay and continue writing or leave the ideas hanging? My back is getting stiff, shall I move? Mmmm this vodka tastes good, shall I have another sip... and so on. As a matter of course, each one of us is in a constant process of making choices and prioritising.

It is a given that there are only 24 hours a day, 7 days a week, and we need to make space for the two main time consumers: sleeping and eating. Together with the ever-increasing and competing demands on the same time limitations, the need and expectation to be effective and efficient are also increasing. The type of choices we make on an almost minute-to-minute basis will have an impact on not only our effectiveness but also our well-being.

Sometimes choosing the order and priority for certain actions is simple. For example, if you are going to take a shower it is more useful to take off your clothes before you step under the flowing water. But with less obvious sequences we can get tempted away from seeing what really needs to be done, or what needs our immediate attention, and what can wait for a minute, an hour, a day, a week or even longer. Daily demands can appear to require an urgent response, particularly in some work set-ups and with, for example, full time parenting. All too often this can result in an action being in 'response to' what we receive as being urgent, whilst neglecting other more important elements in our life. It is helpful to regularly take a moment to look and consider 'the big picture.' Neglect can easily build up and become self-destructive. Seemingly trivial and often elusive moments can turn into a major problem. This could range from keeping up to date with certain business relations, to maintaining your physical health or intimate rapport with your family and friends. The GAP between our self and frequently those who may be the most important people in our lives can stretch to the point of no return.

A particularly ambitious and hard working executive comes to mind. Menno's desire to succeed at work (in a large Dutch company) resulted in him not prioritising effectively enough for every element in his life to flourish. The company demands appeared more urgent and important than the less dramatic daily desires and needs of his family. Reading this I am sure you can guess what I am going to say next... Yes, Menno's wife left him, taking the children with her. He was shocked, devastated, and to escape his grief threw himself even more intensively into his job. About six months later he had functioned so well at work that he was offered a position on the Managing Board. Menno told me that he suddenly realised if he did not take a more active hands-on role with his young children, who no longer lived with him, that their relationship would become little more than a title. His response to the offer was: *"Yes, I would love to accept the position, but only if I can work three and a half days a week. The other one and a half days I want to spend with my children."* To his amazement they accepted. He was delighted, but also saddened by the realisation that in many ways his change of priority had come too late, his marriage was over and with it the daily intimacy of family life.

Menno's initial way of prioritising was probably not simply to do with his character, but also influenced by gender conditioning. Depending on our background and gender we will be encouraged to think certain things have a different order of importance.

Water story

During a session with nine professional women the whole group were sitting in a conference space focussing on Sally. As she walked across the room she accidentally knocked over a glass of water onto one of the tables. The two women close to the spilt water, as their conditioning to tidy up was stronger than their desire to keep their attention on Sally, immediately started mopping up the water. The consequence of them choosing to change their focus of attention to the water was that they missed Sally's 'turning-point learning-moment.' In turn they also missed a learning-moment for themselves. Although we later discussed what had happened, a split in the levels of emotional connection between the group members remained. GAPs in experiential understanding had been created.

Interestingly, we had a similar situation with an all male group. Men are not generally conditioned to tidy up after others, and although they may have experienced a small impulse to mop up the water, they immediately realised it was more important to keep their attention with their colleague. The individual learning plus group understanding and appreciation was therefore at an optimum.

There is no perfect answer to choosing a sequence of events. However, it is helpful to take a moment to think past an action into the possible consequences, as with the women and the glass of water.

Over the years I have noticed that the individuals who dare to make clear choices, and are able to say *"not now"* to last minute requests from an 'important' person or client, gain more personal credibility and often higher leadership positions in an organisation. I believe it is a misplaced sense of responsibility to blindly stick with such dictums as *"The customer always comes first."* What if you have three customers and a family member who are all demanding your attention at the same time? And what about you and your needs? We cannot be all things to all people, and attempting this is a sure way to burn-out.

During the past 25 years, whilst painting and drawing, I have become more and more fascinated by how it is possible to guide the way people look at a canvas. What is the function of a particular line? Is it defining a solid object in the foreground or is it defining the background? By changing our focus or the way we look, we can completely change what we see, as shown by the following well-known image.

Do you choose to see the goblet... 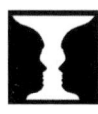 or the two faces?

If you take this idea into your daily interaction it can change the nature of 'the way' and 'the what' you see. This will influence the choice and priority of the actions, which then follow. Sometimes, as in the case of Menno, it is hard to tell what is the most important thing to do. This could be because of: *'Not being able to see the wood for the trees.'* In America the saying is: *'Not being able to see the forest for the trees.'* Interestingly with the English version even with this short saying by changing the interpretation of one word we can create a different perspective: the word 'wood' can mean both a piece of a tree or a group of trees standing together. Therefore transforming the meaning of the saying to the opposite message.

Our perspective on anything can and will change. But at different moments decisions need to be made. There is a big difference between performing semi-decisive reactions or taking a moment to strategise and make a clear choice and action. I have found that the clearer and more decisive a person is in prioritising the importance of the information they are giving, or the action they are taking, the more inspiring they become to their colleagues and friends. It is a leadership skill which gives everyone a moment of clarity and relief from the bombardment of those 'decisions to be made.'

The more clarity we can have with ourselves about what is the best thing to say or decision to be made at a particular moment, the easier it is for others to know where they stand. From this clear point, we can then all proceed to the next choice.

AND-DO-IT
Testing the Knee-Jerk

Take a moment to consider the following questions:

→ Notice what your immediate impulse is when someone asks you to do something.

Does it depend on:
- What the request is?
- What you happen to be doing at the time of being asked?
- What your relationship is with that person?

→ If your boss, client, assistant or friend asks you to do the same thing will your drive for action be the same?

→ Do you have a knee-jerk response into action or do you take a moment to prioritise?

→ Do you become infected by the urgency of other people's desire for your assistance?

Now consider when you ask someone to do something:

DO YOU
→ Request action from others as the need hits you?

OR DO YOU
→ Prioritise by choosing the most important issues?
→ Consider when would be the best time to ask and to do it?
→ Consider who would be the best person to tackle the task?

Experiment with changing any one element of the above. Notice the effect.

AND-DO-IT
Priority Gapping

Note the answers to the following questions
It could help to write them down in four columns.

Which different types of requests, activities and desires do you:

→   Immediately respond to?

→   Wait for the best time to do it?

→   Provoke a dance of procrastination?

→   Repeatedly neglect?

Would the quality of a relationship improve if an action-priority was changed?

Choose one item and make a realistic action plan to make a change: what, how, when.

Sometimes just one small change can have quite a large knock-on effect.

Would this change close an UNDERSTANDING GAP?
JUST DO IT.

2 Flexibility with Holding On & Letting Go

This section includes two AND-DO-ITs
...can help circumvent the vulnerable feelings...

As discussed in the section: Choice – Importance & Priority, during each day we are constantly required to make decisions. The next step is that some of these decisions will require being re-assessed and maybe adjusted or changed completely. We therefore need to be decisive as well as staying flexible enough to adjust.

The passing of time often influences importance and value.

Materially Speaking

A bowl
A big beautiful bowl
Brought back from foreign travels

My dear close friend
Dropped a metal ball
(how irritating)
And the bowl lost a little bit of its edge.
"I don't mind", I said minding.
2 days ago she died
I turned the scarred edge away from the wall
Back into view.

Our accurate insight into the importance of something cannot be foolproof. Therefore to be open and alert to changing a perspective and possibly letting go of a decision or point of view is vital, particularly when it will have an effect on other people. This can appear exceptionally hard to do if we feel our position of authority may be compromised. For example: we may stay with a particular decision too long because we have been taught that to change our mind will be perceived as weak. Sometimes a misplaced sense of pride can compel us to hold on too long to a point of view, or conversely, we change our opinion too quickly because we feel insecure or bullied.

To combine decisiveness with being able to let go can help circumvent the vulnerable feelings, which can happen when others judge, do not agree or do not accept our point of view. In discussions, to be able to adjust one's own standpoint is often an inspiring role model, whereby group thinking and development does not get stuck around one individual's sense of identity.

It is all too easy to muddle how we think others receive one of our ideas, thoughts or actions with our sense of how they perceive us as a whole person. Exploring the letting go action in small moments on a regular basis (examples in the second AND-DO-IT at the end of this section) can help us realise the difference.

Sometimes we do not want to make a decision, because we do not have access to enough information. For complex actions, the idea of the different consequences can be a burden. However, circumstances can sometimes demand action, even when we believe we do not really know enough, in which case a feeling of flexibility is even more important.

To openly accept and declare that: *"This is my best thinking at this moment in time"* **as well as giving yourself the right and flexibility, if you receive more information, to change or adapt, gives you the space to proceed and progress.**

If you keep endorsing the process of visibly holding on and letting go, into the action of decision-making, it also makes it easier for others to be able to declare their position and help close the understanding or agreement GAP. To work with someone who is clear and decisive can be inspiring. To work with someone who is inflexible and who will not let go once they have come to a decision, can feel frustrating and even suffocating as we become a prisoner in their time-freeze.

This holding on and letting go action is fundamental if you want to succeed in many sports. For example: in a match between two world class tennis players, throughout the game they are being extraordinarily decisive, holding on to their technique with strong clear action as they hit the ball and re-position themselves on the tennis court. At the same time they are being extremely flexible, as they receive moment-to-moment information about the other player. To win they need to hold on to their knowledge about the game and their opponent, and at the same time let go of the preconceived ideas of how they think the opponent will play, constantly responding to the moment of the actual interaction. The competition is testing both clarity of choice and flexibility of action with their mind, body and emotions.

We can take this idea of clarity of decision, together with ease and flexibility, into our own physicality on a daily basis. It will support us with the more complex levels of decision-making and also help the congruency of how we are perceived. If your very body is not flexible and with a tight jaw and a frozen upper torso you say, for example, to your team: *"I am open and wish to develop this concept taking everyone's input into consideration,"* people may not believe you because of the mixed message in your rigid body. This in turn may not inspire them to contribute their thoughts and ideas. Similarly, if with a collapsed, passive spine and unfocussed eyes you declare that: *"the team needs to immediately come to a clear decision,"* will it be effective?

When a person walks into a meeting with the kind of physicality described in the first AND-DO-IT at the end of this section, it gives a message that both the action of holding on and letting go with not only thoughts but also in the body can co-exist. They walk the talk.

The effect is one of believability and integrity, which inspires others to contribute their ideas. This same notion can be extended to the voice: the contents of your words need to be supported with the resonance and melody of your voice, so you also talk the talk.

When taking a position of leadership, part of the function is to make clear decisions and hold on to a point of view and then know when to be flexible, let go and change.

Clearly hold on. Clearly let go. Clearly hold on. Clearly let go...

AND-DO-IT
Walk the Talk

Get up and walk around the room or down the corridor exploring the following feelings:

→ My backbone is long, strong and decisive.

→ It is also flexible and twists with ease, with each step.

→ My shoulders are open.

→ My arms are loose and swinging.

→ My hands are heavy, open, with a feeling of letting go.

Backbone = Decisive – strong – holding on

Arms & Hands = Flexible – strong – letting go

AND-DO-IT
Dropping and Placing

→ Pick up a pen (or another small object) – hold it – put it down on the table.

→ Pick up the pen again – hold it – let it go and see it drop to the table.

Notice the different feelings: you may experience a slight change in a sense of ownership – 'this pen belongs to me, it is part of me and mine,' when you place it. Or your feeling of ownership and control towards the pen may change, if you drop it.

Take this idea into the next meeting or conversation you have with one or more people. Experiment with the following three ways of adding an idea to the discussion:

1. 'Carefully place' your idea into the conversation and keep holding on to your point of view.

2. 'Drop' (remember the pen feeling) your idea into the conversation, let go and see what happens to it.

3. 'Drop' your idea into the conversation, let go and see what happens to it. As the discussion continues, decide whether to hold on to the idea again in its original form and restate it, or let go and take hold of the developed idea in its new form.

Any of these interactions could be useful depending on the situation.

3 The Body Physicality & Gesture

This section includes two AND-DO-ITs
...Both genders have their physical "must not, cannot do" blind spots...

From the moment we are born, what we physically look like will have a direct effect on the way people treat and respond to us. As we age we will develop different opinions about our bodies. These opinions, which cement a relationship between ourselves and our physical dialogue with society, are created by certain influencing factors from our environment, including when we are born, where we grow up and live, where we work, our family, friends, gender, race, religion, education and age.

When we meet other people, the information which instantly starts to transmit between us will be our physicality. The immensity of this automatic message system is not to be underestimated; it will have an effect on every interpersonal interaction. Investigating our relationship with our own body can be helpful. I have met very few people who feel completely content with the size, shape, appearance and health of their body. If I talk with young children I find this is usually not the case, then bit by bit something happens to us as social norms and values affect the way we think our bodies should appear in order to be acceptable. These messages are often so subtle that we do not recognise them. In many western so-called more liberal cultures, the pressures for females in particular to have a certain bodily appearance are relentless. A quick list of female body-parts being assessed as acceptable (and sexual enough) could look like this:

→ length, colour and texture of hair,
→ size and position of ears,
→ shape and hairiness of eyebrows,
→ shape and size of eyes,
→ length and thickness of eyelashes,
→ shape of cheekbones,
→ length, size and shape of nose,
→ shape and size of mouth,

- thickness of lips,
- straightness and colour of teeth,
- shape and clarity of jaw line,
- amount of lines or 'wrinkles' on face and neck,
- length and slimness of neck,
- shape of shoulders,
- hairiness of armpits,
- shape of upper arm,
- size of wrists,
- size of hands,
- size, length and shape of fingers,
- length and shape of fingernails,
- size and shape of breasts,
- size, shape and possible erectness of nipples,
- circumference of waist,
- flatness of stomach,
- circumference of hips,
- length and shape of thighs,
- length and shape of calves,
- hairiness of 'bikini' line,
- hairiness of legs,
- shape of knees,
- size of ankles,
- size of feet,
- shape of toes,
- shape of toenails,
- comparative proportions of the previous items with each other,
- smoothness and colour of skin over whole body,
- height and weight of complete body structure.

At any moment during the day if you live in a town or watch television you can see some kind of advertising making a comment about one or many of the above female body-parts.

Yesterday evening during an advertisement intermission on television, yet again I saw a half naked, glamorous, blond nymph writhing almost to the point of orgasm. Apparently this is the kind of woman you could become if you use a certain perfume. Scary. If this type of commercial was a one off, we would laugh at the fairy tale. However, it is not the exception but the rule. The relentless pumping out of a certain narrow ideal of physical femaleness is a tyranny. And even if we intellectually attempt to disregard these images, they keep gnawing away at both men and women's bodily desires and expectations.

A similar list for males could be:
→ height,
→ head hair (or lack of it),
→ shape of nose,
→ strength of jaw,
→ hair on face,
→ size and muscles of shoulders,
→ muscles on upper arms,
→ size and strength of hands,
→ hair on chest,
→ muscles on chest,
→ size of belly,
→ presence of 6 pack,
→ size of penis,
→ distribution of hair over whole body.

I suspect we could make this list longer. But it is clear that whilst both men and women are under pressure to change body size and shape, the pressure on women is greater. The notion that women are more accepting of men's bodies (as they are) is also present.

All or some of the above assessments are at play even before we think about our choice of clothes. The clothing decision will probably be related to an event, gender, income and the socio-political position which an individual is wishing to project. Both genders have a different repertoire. In business, the man's choice although rather restricted is clear: a shirt (usually white or pastel colour), a tie (main area of possibly adventurous self expression), a dark coloured suit and flat shoes. Sometimes jeans are permitted. Usually everything except the shoes will be loose fitting (so their body shape will not be under scrutiny).

Women are not protected by the clarity of the business suit as their only option. They have a much greater choice of how they could clothe themselves. This can be positive if considered strategically. In daily business life I see women who habitually wear figure hugging, physically restrictive variations of t-shirts, blouses, jackets, skirts, dresses and trousers. They seem oblivious to the fact that many of their male colleagues, quite understandably, are focussing on and distracted by their breasts, crotch, buttocks and legs. And then these women become confused when they are not taken seriously, or are given attention solely based on sexual attraction rather than their knowledge and ideas. Yet when I ask groups of professional women if they have ever seen a male jogger who is wearing Lycra sportsshorts, whereby the details of his penis are clearly displayed, they easily agree that this can be distracting, to say the least! There are different schools of thought concerning the way a professional woman should dress to be powerful and effective, and these opinions can turn out to be formulaic and personally inhibiting. For example, recently a female Vice President of a listed company to my amazement explained: *"If you want to be taken seriously as a woman in business you have to wear very high heeled shoes."*

It is worthwhile experimenting and then reflecting on the impact certain clothing can have, both on your own physical agility as well as on another person's assumptions about you.

If we consider eastern cultures there is also a difference between what men and women are encouraged or permitted to wear. The similarity to the west is that female clothing will usually have some kind of restrictive effect on the woman's ability to move. For example, in India it is common to see a woman in a sari working in the fields or on a building site. For the western outsider this can look quite elegant and picturesque, but for the woman in question, although she has had a lifetime learning how to navigate physical agility within those yards of cloth, she has clearly less physical freedom than her male counterpart. Other types of female physical restriction occur in some interpretations of Islam, when women wear variations on the Hijab (headscarf), Chador (a full body cloak), Niqab (veil) and Burqa (full body covering). Suffice to say, fashion, culture and religion have created many complex and often restrictive rules on the way males and females are encouraged or allowed to dress themselves.

Regardless of dress code and personal taste, how others perceive our physical presence will be dramatically affected by the way each one of us inhabits our own body. The way a person 'lives' inside their body can have a remarkable effect on how others see the same vital statistics.

We contain space (inside our bodies) and we take up space (outside our bodies). For various reasons many people collapse in on themselves, making the space inside their body smaller. This can be in the form, to name a few points, of a passive collapsed spine (including the neck), slumped shoulders, tight elbows, clasped hands, locked knees and feet close together. The effect on your body is that the skeleton, musculature and internal organs cannot work as well as they should. To others, you will appear squeezed and collapsed, and with a subconscious empathy they in turn may take on this feeling.

If you cannot remember your first steps walking, perhaps you can think of a small child you know and their first steps. The child will probably give out an expression of joy and excitement as they become able to walk without support from someone else. The ability to move through space independently of another person is a life skill and pleasure. If we feel secure and unthreatened as a child, our physical impulse will often be to stretch out our arms, jump freely in the air, run and skip around to the limits of any space we are in. This is in juxtaposition with the pleasure of receiving physical support from others, whether it is holding hands, linking arms or simply cuddling up to someone. But too much having to lean or being leant on can become debilitating, conversely too much time alone on our own two feet can become lonely or isolating. It is interesting to observe how often people are drawn to leaning on things and themselves, rather than taking space and standing on their own two feet. When you are sitting behind a table do you lean on it? If you are standing, do you lean against nearby furniture or a wall or by crossing your arms literally lean on yourself?

There is a difference between leaning becoming a passive collapsed action or leaning and at the same time maintaining your physical energy. For example, if you are at this moment sitting behind a table, lean forwards on your arms using as few muscles as possible to keep your balance, maybe even lean your chin on your hand. Now to change this into an 'active lean' starting from the base of your spine slowly use all the muscles in your back until your torso is fully lengthened while your arms are lightly resting on the table.

If we see someone who is giving independent original thinking and they are leaning and physically collapsed the messages we hear will be in conflict with the ones we see.

Recently it occurred to me that there is another reassuring feeling which may happen when we either touch ourselves by crossing our arms or when our body touches something or someone. In each case we become more aware of where the circumference of our body ends and the rest of the world begins. If I am not leaning on myself (hanging in my hips with crossed arms) or leaning on furniture or another person, I experience a different connection with my environment. This can be described as a feeling of limitlessness.

As you sit reading this section notice the difference in the physical sensation of where your skin is touching either an object, the chair you are sitting on, your clothes, other skin on your body, or where your skin is only touching the air. Note that if there is no wind current in the air it may be harder to define where your body stops and where the air begins. Consider next time you lean on something if it is because you want to feel where your body stops and the rest of the universe begins.

When standing, even the simple act of placing the feet shoulder-width apart can be surprisingly confrontational. Men may feel over-dominant or military and women can feel inelegant and 'un-female'. Both genders have their physical 'must not, cannot do' blind spots. And yet when, for example, they do try out this wider foot position, colleagues both male and female remark on how strong and relaxed it looks. Not to mention that from this stance the action of walking is much easier and more dynamic.

The amount of space we allow ourselves to take up outside our body will probably depend on the situation and once again our conditioning. There have been aerial view studies made of children playing in playgrounds. They observed that more often than not, the boys will be taking up large amounts of the space in the central area playing physically demonstrative games such as football, whilst the girls will occupy the edges of the playground, with games involving smaller physical movements. Some of this may be explained by the difference in the muscular and skeletal development of the two sexes. Some will be gender conditioning. Many males are encouraged and are used to taking up physical space, whereas many females are not. This is easy to observe in a random group of people sitting in a concert, airport or train station. More often than not males will have their legs and arms wide apart and females will have their legs and arms crossed or held in tight to their body.

From an early age many young females will be encouraged to be pretty, neat, clean and graceful, whereas young males may often be encouraged to be physically demonstrative, adventurous and strong. If they get muddy, scratched and their clothes become ripped, oh well he's a boy. If a female as a young girl likes to climb trees and play rough she may be referred to as a **tomboy**, i.e. a female form of maleness. The term **tomboy** can be traced back in England to the 16th century, when it was used to describe a *'rude and boisterous boy'*, a *'bold and immodest woman'*, a *'girl who acts with the spirit of a boy'* or a *'rude and sexually uncontrolled girl – a strumpet'*. More recently, the shortened slang term *'Tom'* meaning prostitute is sometimes used by officers in the London police force.

If males behave in even a slightly physically 'female' way, they may be labelled as being a **sissy**. It could be something as small as a boy being hesitant to do something physically risky and his friends give him the negative label of *"sissy!"* **Sissy** is a pejorative for a boy or man to indicate that he fails to behave according to the traditional male gender role. Generally, it implies a lack of courage as well as being used to label interests seen as un-masculine. Other similar terms include *'femboy'* and *'pussy'*.

So for both genders to be likened to the typical physical mannerisms and behaviour patterns of the other sex often has a negative connotation.

Concerning physical risk taking, within a random group of professional men, when asked many of them will have broken a bone or ripped a tendon or muscle once if not countless times during their life. With a group of professional women this is less common and even rare. These males from an early age are used to taking physical risks and surviving injury. It makes me wonder if this reflects on the ease of solo risk-embracing decision-making in the corporate world, which seems to be a more attractive way of operating for males, versus the more cautious and often consensus model frequently used by women.

In a western culture most people will have experienced some kind of physical training throughout their childhood, be it in sport or dance. As we get older many adults realise the importance of regular athletic movement and belong to a gym or sports club. Unfortunately the effective use of our bodies is rarely taught well. In my local park I regularly see joggers running in such a way that if they continue, they will over time cause physical injury to themselves.

Not only during 'sportive' attempts to maintain health but also back in the workplace it is useful for a professional communicator to re-sensitize themselves with the moment-to-moment needs of their body. This is not only noticing the necessity to eat, drink, rest, breathe and visit the toilet, but also realising when the emotional tension of a meeting has transformed itself into, for example, tight shoulders or a stiff neck. First we need to have the recognition and then the motivation and knowledge to do something about it. If we do nothing about the daily physical tension build-up the result can be exhausting for the individual and confusing for others. For example, if you have developed a stiff back and angry facial expression due to sitting in a traffic jam and you carry this into a meeting, the people in the meeting may misinterpret your physical presence and think you are reacting negatively to something they have said or done. An UNDERSTANDING GAP is created.

Physical tension build-up can have an even longer history. I recently had a meeting with a rather tall man who when he stood up to greet me was stooping over. I could (mis)interpret this in several ways. *'He is bending down towards me because: he is being condescending, he thinks I cannot handle 'all' of him, he lacks confidence, he has a backache, he is tired, he wishes he was not as tall as he actually is...'* Later when I left I pointed this out to him and he answered: *"Do you know how many times I have hit my head when I walk though a doorway?"* So he had developed a permanent posture related to passing under a low doorway. I asked him to notice that as we were talking he was standing in the middle of a large room, with a high ceiling and no possible danger of him bumping the top of his head. He smiled.

A physical stance which many people get drawn into, particularly when they have a strong desire to be understood, is with their shoulders slumped and their head jutting forwards. It is as if by pushing forwards in this manner, their audience will be closer to the thoughts in the speaker's head. The chest becomes collapsed and curved inwards and the back of the neck shortened. This position is similar to a bigger action when we gasp with shock: our jaw swings down, throwing our head backwards, and our shoulders spring upwards and cave in, in a position of defence. If you have ever seen two cats fighting, the weaker animal as it goes into submission and retreat will take up a similar physical shape. This position occurs with many animals when retreating from a physical conflict. Since our origins are also rooted here, this kind of physicality can give a subliminal message of defence and submission to the people we are attempting to communicate with. Thus the intention GAP becomes huge.

Remembering the posture of any young person who has recently learnt to walk you will see that their chest is open (suggesting an open heart) and their head is balanced beautifully on their neck with the back of the neck being long, open and flexible (this is the main highway for the nervous system from the brain to the rest of the body). We will feel an instinctive trust towards the child. If an adult has this open easy physicality it will create a similar response in others. As the child grows and tensions of the civilising process mount the collapsing very often starts and the physically defensive posture becomes entrenched.

To counterbalance the upper-body collapse and thrust, when you talk to other people, try developing the private image that you first give the message to yourself. We cannot give something away that we have not owned. With this background thought your message will resonate out of all of you, rather than just words plus a disembodied head pivoting forwards.

In this context, it is helpful to keep thinking:
(1) I am three-dimensional. (2) Bring the audience to me.

These two thoughts are abstract but the effect can be that you then communicate with your whole body. It can enable you to make a sensitive space between yourself and the people you are talking with, rather than pushing your personality and physicality into their face. In turn it gives others the room to physically position themselves according to their individual preference.

Gestures
Another reason why it is useful to not carry muscle tension residue from our day-to-day life around with us is that a large part of our communication vocabulary takes the form of physical gesture and movement. Clearly if the face is frozen in one permanently tense position, it will prevent any other spontaneous facial expression from happening. The frozen expression is what is transmitted as a message, whatever the underlying emotion may be. Have you come across people who talk as if their face is a mask giving the effect that they are either half dead or working for the FBI? It is genuinely hard to de-code what they really mean.

The same idea translates to any part of the body. If for some reason you are experiencing a physical tension and you do not get rid of it, then even if you wish to enhance your words with physical movement, not much will happen. Your movement will be restricted and incomplete. If you say to a group of people: *"We have infinite possibilities"* (and you genuinely believe and feel this), your arms may give some kind of outward movement to support the words. However, if your shoulders are stiff and you always keep your arms tightly held into your torso then the movement will probably be contained and self conscious. As this movement is restricted you will be giving a contradictory message with your body. The result will be that the people with whom you are talking will, on some level, not believe or trust you. If you say that same statement with loose easy arms and shoulders, you will probably make a wide throwing gesture truly illustrating infinity. The result will be that your spoken message is enhanced and supported by your body in subtle and unique movements. As there are few tensions the movement is also more likely to have a spontaneous quality. People will trust you and more easily remember what you have said.

To regularly let go of outdated and unrelated body habits and tensions will not only refresh our personal energy but also help to close the UNDERSTANDING GAPs.

For finding physical grounding, balancing, negative tension release and awareness you could take some classes in Tai Chi, Alexander technique, Feldenkrais, yoga or some other form of bodywork. This could be a pleasurable experience as well as a valuable investment.

But for now...

AND-DO-IT
Tension Clean-Up

Check through your body:

→ wiggle your toes
→ circle your ankles
→ shake your legs
→ swing your hips
→ twist your spine
→ throw out your arms
→ circle your shoulders
→ nod and shake your head
→ rub your hands
→ stretch your face
→ loosen your jaw

Notice if any area feels stiff or locked. if so, spend a bit more time moving that part, until the tension has shifted.

Do the above any time, any place, with bigger or smaller movements depending on where you are.

If you are in one physical position either sitting or standing for some time, change, move, stretch.

Our bodies are not designed to stay rigidly still for long periods of time.

AND-DO-IT

Wide Feet - Active Standing

→ Stand up with your feet as far apart as the width of your shoulders (probably slightly wider than your hips).

→ Make sure your knees are loose, do not lock at any time.

→ Use, in particular, your strong thigh and buttock muscles.

→ Keep an easy and steady breath.

Then Slowly

→ Lean as far forward onto your toes as you can without falling – notice which muscles are working the most to maintain this position – slowly bring your weight back to a central distribution.

→ Repeat the same action this time leaning backwards.

→ Repeat the same action leaning to the right.

→ Repeat the same action leaning to the left.

Each time you return your weight to a central position see how effortlessly you can maintain this by finding an easy balance.

4 Space

This section includes three AND-DO-ITs
...Most people only know the substantial...

The word space is used in plenty of different contexts, from the extreme of a global competition to explore beyond planet earth in the case of the *'space race'* to a personal cry for a bit of peace and quiet with room to have one's own thoughts, *"Get out of my space"... "Give me space..."*

Mental Space
Many of us are bombarded with visual and sound information every day. Even though it may regularly not feel like it, we adjust what we allow into our consciousness. We choose when to read our emails, put on television, answer our phone, listen to music or open the newspaper. To protect ourselves from over-stimulation when we walk down the street, we could even consider wearing blinkered glasses and earplugs. Perhaps a bit extreme, but if we are being continually open and receptive to all the stimulation around us, it can sometimes feel insane. With advertising on television for example: in the case of a product or with a music-clip, the speed of information is often extremely fast and punchy; we are being bullied into receiving it. To an increasing number of people this aggressive stimulation is becoming addictive. And the widespread zapping between one form of electronic media and another has become to some even compulsive. But it is perceived, certainly from the point of view of a western teenager, as normal. There is quite some discussion about how effective or even healthy this amount of stimulation is. Only time will tell.

There is an additional concern, which is that as people become accustomed and even addicted to being able to communicate with each other any time any place and do so 24/7, they are losing the ability to be alone. If this limitless contact is then interrupted, it can become a frighteningly lonely place to be. To be on your own does not have to be lonely. Depending on your religious beliefs, each one of us is ultimately alone. It is valuable to re-visit and regularly savour this experience to understand that being by yourself can be productive, pleasurable and even adventurous.

Appreciation and desire for personal mental space is individual. By keeping up to date with our own presumed requirements we may find more variation or flexibility than we realised.

Illustration story

For several years I earned my living as an illustrator. My drawings were often humorous and cartoon-like with a spiky and spontaneous visual style. I would usually be given a week or two by the commissioning paper or magazine depending on the complexity and quantity of their request. I would always go through a lengthy process of reading the article and then letting the imagery settle in the back of my mind. Whilst I played with drawing endless visual ideas, I would throw the obvious interpretations out of my system until more interesting ideas evolved. This took time and I *'needed'* the space to let it float. To give you an overview, for one drawing of about the size of an A4 page it would take me on and off about a week. This would be interspersed with parallel visual activities including painting and drawing several other illustrations in the same time frame.

Then I had a baby. In between one of Ruby's feeds or sleeps and the next there were short time slots which were often filled with basic activities, to keep the household running. And yet I was also getting illustration commissions. Instead of a week of contemplation and exploration, I now had a few interrupted hours. It was interesting how quickly I re-adjusted my process and within this new short time frame managed to produce the work. To my surprise the ideas were there and the quality of the drawings was, perhaps, even better.

So funnily enough in this example I needed less mental space and time than I had become accustomed to. The reverse can also be true. Sometimes if I have an overload of 'commitments' which I believe need immediate attention, it can be more productive to stop and take a break. I have found when I then return to the tasks in hand, my thinking is clearer and sharper. Although I may initially take more time, it will probably end up saving time as the quality of my action will be high enough, not to have to repeat or re-do. **Taking mental space can give space.**

It is worth adding that my ability to complete the drawings in a couple of hours was also because I had the knowledge and experience in my fingertips; I had been drawing and painting on an almost daily basis for quite some years previous to becoming a mother. The more we repeat activities the better we often become at them. This in turn gives us more options with how much time and space we may need to invest in the action. In his book *Outliers* Malcom Gladwell devotes a chapter to his theory of the 10,000 Hour Rule. He arrives at the conclusion that given a particular talent or aptitude, personal excellence will occur in an individual after approximately 10,000 hours of practising that particular skill.

Someone once pointed out to me that part of the process of painting is often about *'not'* painting. It concerns the amount of time you spend just sitting, staring at a blank wall, daring to dwell in the so called empty space of your mind. I definitely recognise this and would like to extend the concept to any process requiring innovative thinking. Those around you may think you are doing nothing and sometimes I have even made that judgement on myself. The work ethic is so strong that many individuals can easily feel they are wasting time by seemingly *'doing nothing.'*

And then there is the commonly described *'deadline syndrome.'* If you have from Monday to Friday to do something you may well end up doing it on Friday. And yet if you are told you have to do the same thing in one day your response may be, *"Impossible! I need more time..."* and then you manage to do it anyway. Sometimes the perceived need for mental space is more to do with habit than necessity, as in the illustration story. Sometimes it is a real need; the time apparently 'wasted' in procrastination is actually being well used.

Keep identifying and being proactive with taking the personal space you think you need. I like the question, *"Are you living your life or is life living you?"* **If you do not literally demand the mental space you want or need: to think, listen to music, go for a walk or even sleep, it will not necessarily be given to you.**

When you are talking to and working with a group of people, notice how much variation of thinking space the individuals, as well as the group, may need. For example, do they need time to think about your idea, or are they immediately ready for your next thought? The complexity of the subject matter, the true urgency of the process, and the individuals concerned will all play their part in your assessment.

Consider the two words: **wait** and **weight**. If we give time and mental space around communicating certain ideas and feelings by **waiting**, we can give more **weight** to our content and the way we are received and perceived. The patience required in being able to **wait** can be determined by our emotional habits, which we may feel we cannot guide or choose. Repeatedly people will defend these habits: *"That's me, that's who I am, I always feel and react like that and there is nothing I can do about it..."*. This is not the case, we have a choice. Jill Bolte Taylor in her book, *My Stroke of Insight*, explains how many emotional responses, although triggered automatically in a certain bodily limbic system, will after 90 seconds be *'flushed out through our blood stream'*. Thereafter if for example we remain angry it is because we have *'chosen to let that circuit continue to run'*.

'Response-ability' means that after the first 90 seconds of feeling an emotion, if the emotion continues then it moves from being an automatic response-emotion to an emotional state which we choose to maintain.

Physical Space

Depending on where we grow up we all form different preferences for physical spaces. If you grow up in the countryside with a lot of space around you then to be in the city may feel crowded, even claustrophobic. If you spend your childhood in a city and have, for example, to regularly use public transport where to be squashed up against other people is normal, then to walk in the countryside may feel uncomfortably spacious, even daunting. I grew up in a house in London, which had quite big rooms and high ceilings. I am also tall; I feel comfortable in large rooms and constricted in small spaces. I have friends who would prefer to live in a house with small 'cosy' rooms. If we recognise these preferences it can add to our spatial sensitivity.

Recently I gave a lecture to a group of about 80 university students. The hall was run down, cold, with low lighting and hollow acoustics. The students were sitting on uncomfortable collapsible chairs pushed close together in rows, with a central aisle and a pillar right in the middle of the cramped front area where I was supposed to stand and talk. As I gave the lecture I walked around the space and between the audience, attempting to open up the spatial barrier between me and them. I had to work hard to form any kind of relationship with the audience due to the unwelcoming physical restrictions of the space.

If you ever have to give some kind of lecture or presentation, if possible visit the place beforehand or arrive early. When a furniture setup is working against your easy physical access to the audience, see if you can change it to suit your needs. When this is not possible at least be mentally prepared to focus on other communication skills, for example the way you use your voice.

Often in the offices of large companies people are required to have meetings where there is hardly space to swing a cat. In many organisations it is recognised that space equals status, the bigger the office, the better the view and number of windows, the higher the ranking. More square metres cost more money. If you are meeting in a small or overcrowded space make sure that it does not make you small either in your movements or your thinking. If the room is large do not let it inhibit you.

Light can also have a dramatic effect on a space, making it feel larger or smaller than its actual square metres. If bright sunlight is coming from one side of the room then it will probably be hard to see the faces of the people sitting with their backs to the window, unless there is also some artificial light coming from another direction as a counterbalance. When I have a meeting in such a space, I consciously decide if it is more useful for people to easily see my face or the other way round. I then sit accordingly.

Similarly it is worthwhile considering where to sit at a large table in juxtaposition with the other person(s) present. And where is the door? Some people feel uncomfortable or distracted if their back is to the door, some not. Keep aware of all the possibilities a certain space has to offer you. Give yourself time to not only analyse but also sense your personal reaction to a room or space. Our feelings related to different kinds of spaces are not necessarily logical or reasonable. But they will definitely affect the ease in which we interact with our self and others.

The following quote from the Esoteric Tao Teh Ching by Hua-Ching Ni has often helped me to appreciate space from a different perspective:

> Although supported by substantial spokes and wheels,
>> it is the insubstantial empty space
>> which makes a cart useful.
> Although supported by substantial pot-earth,
>> it is the insubstantial hollow space
>> which makes earthenware useful.
> Although supported by substantial material
>> of doors, windows, and walls,
>> it is the insubstantial space
>> created by the windows, doors and walls
>> which make a house useful.
> What is substantial offers the benefit,
>> but the real use of a thing
>> comes from what is insubstantial.
> Most people only know the substantial,
>> they do not know the true value
>> is in the insubstantial.

It is not simply the material delineation of space around us (ceilings, walls, tables, chairs, windows) but the insubstantial space between us, which plays a dynamic role in communicating. How close or far away we are from each other – the physical space, which we negotiate between us – is both personal and cultural. To place this sensitively in any interaction can have an effect on everyone. For example: in a meeting to sit or stand just that bit too close or too far away from the person you are attempting to explain your ideas to, can have consequences. Too close may create an invasion of their privacy, too far away may create an impression of disinterest or even arrogance. In either case a successful pitch will be jeopardised. The subtleties of how to position ourselves are personal and individual: we can usually sense the acceptable or necessary distance on a subconscious, intuitive level. It is useful to keep this in mind and even strategise with the possibilities.

One question, which is regularly voiced, is how to know in which way to greet one another. As the mix of a cross cultural society increases, the way we do this and the physical space involved in each action becomes less apparent. To kiss, embrace, shake hands, bow...and then the subtleties of any of these actions, for example: one kiss on the cheek or three? They are all moments where our spatial relationship with each other can give a lot of information. It will build on or hinder the effectiveness of how we then proceed as the UNDERSTANDING GAP is accentuated or diminished.

A familiar experience for me is when I meet a client and they give me the *'super strong handshake.'* Some time during their career it has probably been explained: *'if you are a strong decisive businessman or businesswoman, then you must give a clear strong handshake.'* The result is pain, and as I am not a masochist, I get a feeling of wanting to distance myself from them. The finger-cracking grip happens because a vital piece of information has been omitted. The strength of the clasp should be decided not only from your own point of view but also taking into consideration the feel, size and strength of the other person's hand, as well as the corporate and country culture. At which point you can together create a collaborative strength, whereby neither person is crushing nor dominating the other. And then there is the length of time of the shake, the standing distance between the two people, the eye contact, facial expression, the ease and flexibility of the arm and shoulder... we will intuitively pick up on some or all of this information.

When someone has to give a speech, a question which comes up is: *"When is it best to walk and when to stand still?"* How often have you seen someone talking on the phone and continuously walking around the room at the same time, as if their thoughts are attached to their feet? Similarly, when people give a speech in front of an audience, they may often pace up and down. If someone never arrives and stands still, when they walk from one place/space to another it can have a visually exhausting and fragmenting effect on the people who are listening. This in turn often influences which words they choose to use and the delivery becomes an endless stream of information. In English if we describe someone as holding their ground (probably originating from the battle grounds of history) it means they are keeping a firm hold of their point of view. If you decide to use physical space when you are communicating, remember to have clear moments of standing still between the walking. Also keep in mind to hold your ground, stand still, whilst you are receiving a question from someone, as well as when giving an answer. It will help clarity and belief. It is amazing how often people answer a question or describe a thought whilst walking backwards away from the group. This gives the impression that the person is walking away from their words, and can create the effect that the audience, not consciously knowing why, will doubt the speaker's integrity.

Using physical space in a variety of clear and sensitive ways, considering both the environment around you as well as the space between yourself and others, will enable you to observe more accurately, whilst making sure your thoughts land effectively.

Earlier in this section I identified mental space, concerning the thinking time we give to ourselves and others, and how choosing to vary this timing impacts on emotional, creative and thinking effectiveness. These elements are often woven together with physical/spatial skills. If we use them with consideration and strategy it could avoid the people we are talking with or even ourselves becoming all 'spaced out'. (mmm…could not resist that one)

AND-DO-IT
Mental Spacing

→ Notice and change the amount of mental space you give yourself to think about or do something.

→ Spend conscious time considering the mental space you give others. This could take the form of listening longer without adding your point of view, delegating without micro-managing...

Change and challenge your familiar patterns.

AND-DO-IT
Spatial Dancing

→ Get to recognise which kind of spaces put you at ease and which do not.

→ Notice other people's reactions to different spaces.

→ Notice how close you choose to be to other people when standing and sitting. Vary these distances.

→ What can you do to make a space more appealing to your personal preference?

→ Keep changing the place/space where you choose to sit at the dinner table at home.

→ Keep changing where you sit in a regular meeting room at work – break the habit. Notice that by simply sitting somewhere else you can change the dynamics of your relationship with whoever you are talking with.

→ When sitting behind a table, change the space between yourself and the table in order to give yourself enough space to gesture and move.

AND-DO-IT

The Handshake

During the next weeks note how you greet people.
If the handshake is appropriate experiment with the following ideas:

→ **Strength** of grasp: put your attention on receiving this information from the other person. Aim at finding a strength which suits both of you.

→ **Length of time** of shaking: make sure your arm and shoulder are flexible and then come to a common sensitivity as to when to stop shaking.

→ **Space between** yourself and others: alter the standing distance.

→ **Eye contact:** Note emotional clarity – Do you experience that 'click' moment, do they really see you? How long do their eyes stay with you?

5 Eyes & Contact

This section includes two AND-DO-ITs
...and then rolling our eyes to the ceiling...

Have you ever felt the sensation that someone is looking at you? You turn in the direction where you felt the look was coming from, and sure enough come eyeball to eyeball with that person. Even though you had not initially seen them, you felt their gaze. If I ask this question I cannot think of a time when someone has not known what I was talking about, whatever the size of the group. There has been quite some research on this phenomenon, and if it specifically interests you, you may enjoy reading Rupert Sheldrake's book *The Sense of Being Stared At*.

The following exercise explores this sensation: a group of people are asked to turn their backs towards one colleague, the speaker. Then as the speaker reads a text, the rest of the group are asked to raise their hand, when or if they experience an increased and stronger sense of connection and understanding with the speaker. The speaker is asked to keep changing their gaze towards each of the audience members as they speak, even though the audience cannot see them. Like clockwork as the speaker talks and looks towards the back of an individual, that person will raise their hand. The speaker is amazed as time and again this interaction is proven.

Two things are happening here: firstly the listening person will sense the extra attention of the look, and secondly the voice will, for that moment, be literally projected towards the individual and they will hear the difference. Our sound perception is much more finely tuned than we may be aware of. Your voice will specifically go towards the person or people you are looking at.

Regularly clients then ask, *"But what about large groups or audiences? I cannot possibly look at everyone at the same time!"* With large audiences a speaker will often look at no-one specifically, as they feel there are too many people and therefore there is no point. Or they fixate on the few people they know, or the ones they believe are the most important. The way to give everyone in the room a sense that you are looking at them is to have specific eye contact with several different people spread throughout the whole room. Interestingly, the people around that one person will feel as if you are looking at them as well. In all cases, ranging from an individual to a large group, if you speak to your paper, the projection screen, your laptop, out the window, the floor, the ceiling or your breakfast cereal, those places or objects will receive the majority of your message.

Only a few days ago a shy young man said to me, "*I am so happy*" (to me) "*to meet you*" (to his paper on the table). The effect of his message was that he was happy to meet his paper. What he did was very common. People will often start off their idea looking towards the person or people they are talking to and then before they have finished speaking, as their mind jumps ahead, they will look to their notes or perhaps the floor even though there is no information there. Often the audience will then simply stop listening. The reception or exchange of the information will be scattered and incomplete. The GAP becomes enormous.

If we imagine that I am throwing a ball to you, it seems obvious, if I want you to be able to catch it, then I need to look in your direction. And I need you to look at me. If I do not look at you, the likelihood of me succeeding will be random and may lead to one of the following reactions:

→ You wondering why I was throwing you the ball.
→ You trying to catch my attention first, so that I really throw the ball in such a way that you will be able to catch it.
→ You not daring to interrupt me and then overstretching yourself, in an attempt to catch the ball.
→ You not bothering to try and catch it.

Yet with speaking how often do we consider the necessity to maintain active eye contact throughout the whole interaction? To give the thought and see the spoken thought land, be received and absorbed by the listener.

Have you ever been in a meeting or conversation and noticed that not only is the person talking never looking at you, but a glazed look has come over their eyes? They appear blind as their full attention gets sucked into themselves and their own thoughts. They forget that they are actually speaking those thoughts and presumably wanting someone else to hear and understand them.

It is frequently noted that the eyes are windows to the soul. How often in songs and poetry is the action of looking *into* someone's eyes described? As if through the eyes we enter the person. We begin to know who they are. People will definitely believe and trust you more readily if your eyes stay open, curious and focussed on them. You can communicate well if you are, and they feel you are, actually seeing them and their reactions as you talk.

The same goes for the person who is listening. If they show interest, with their eyes looking towards the speaker, it is encouraging and even inspiring for the person who is attempting to tell their story. The reverse is almost more powerful, in a negative way. As an audience member, just with our eyes, we can indicate boredom or disinterest, by simply looking out of the window, glancing at our watch or constantly looking at and writing (unrelated) notes. We can do even more destructive eye movements, for example catching the eye of someone else in the room and then rolling our eyes to the ceiling. Or as the speaker talks directly to us, avoiding eye contact by sliding our look to one side (a popular 'eye action' with school kids to dismiss a classmate or even one of their teachers). So the listener has a lot of power: just with their eyes they can create many positive or negative effects.

There are theories about what it means if someone looks away in different directions whilst talking or thinking. Do they look up, down, to the right or left, do they blink, stare or avoid your gaze? Different cultures have different eye etiquettes, many of which are complex and meaningful. But if you start to approach eye movement in a formulaic way, if you use one of these gospels of interpretation, you may come to useless and even damaging conclusions about friends or colleagues. Keep informed about the culture you are in and where the people come from that make up the group, certainly take this into consideration but also keep an open mind. And if someone has a repeated, for example, seemingly dismissive eye movement, ask them about it. They may not even realise they are doing it.

Of course when we are talking we cannot constantly maintain eye contact, so when and how should we look away and how can we do it and yet maintain a connection with each other? **Stay in the zone.**

A way to keep a sense of eye contact whilst moving your eyes away from someone is to **stay in the zone** with your eyes. Meaning: whenever you are talking (and for a lot of the time also as a listener) keep your eye focus in line with everyone else's eyes in the room. Either looking into someone else's eyes or keeping your gaze on the same general plane of the group's eyes. In this way, whether you are talking, listening, or thinking about a reply or your next idea, you maintain a sense of connection with your eyes. The larger the group and variation of how people may be sitting and/or standing, the more wide-ranging this expanse will be. **Staying in the zone** with your eyes gives people the feeling you are interested in them and aware of them, as well as what is being talked about. It will help focus and concentration.

If you are the speaker, **staying in the zone** with your eyes also makes it much harder for someone to email or text during a meeting. Some people say they can email and listen simultaneously. Of course we probably all can, but the quality of receiving spoken information whilst at the same time going in and out of an email text is questionable. For many people technology is extremely seductive, maybe because it can give an illusion of high activity. But the more you challenge others to stay with their focus on you and what you are saying, constantly scanning the room and gathering up the attention as if with a fishing net, the more everyone will actually hear your ideas effectively and efficiently. Time is saved.

If you really see the people you are talking with and give yourself moments to absorb the information given by slight nods, questioning frowns and knowing smiles, it will feed you. Firstly because you will experience the contact GAP closing on an emotional level and secondly it could give you indicators to move on to the next point, repeat, cut to the chase or get the hell out of there.

It is useful to realise in groups, that there will be a temptation to focus on certain people. The following types tend to have a magnetic quality:
→ The person you believe is the most important or powerful.
→ The person you feel is the most positive or who is your friend and ally.
→ The most negative member who keeps asking awkward questions.
→ Someone who you find sexually attractive.
→ Anyone who asks a question.
   Remember to include and give your reply to the whole group.

And then all too often the following people may be forgotten:
→ The most junior or the perceived least important member of the group.
→ The person who does not often speak.
→ The person who does not appear to be interested.
→ The person out of your easy vision, possibly sitting beside you, or very near to you.
→ Someone you do not like or who you feel intimidated by.

The ability to maintain balancing the thinking inside your head, with keeping your eyes alert, looking out and actually seeing everyone, is not to be underestimated. By regularly practising and including this element in your conversations, you can help it become second nature.

Largely because of our education, many people's attention and thinking tends to be run by the left hemisphere of the brain, the analytical part. To become more familiar with looking and seeing without feeling compelled to analyse, give yourself short missions to notice different things that you see.
For example:
Today I will notice the colour and texture of everyone's hair!
Today I will notice where the light is coming from in every room I spend time in.

In most cases it is worth seeing and noticing as much as possible…

Cat

The cat it spat
And then it shat
Exactly where I laid the mat
That
You just wiped your feet on.

AND-DO-IT

Testing the Pull to See 'It' Land

Complete the action of each point and then read the connected question (*in italics*).
Proceed to the next action (possibly lay a piece of paper over the following points or ask someone to instruct you)

→ Pick up a pen or small object and throw it with the aim of hitting another object in the room.

Notice when you stopped being engaged in the action: when you threw it or when you saw it land?
Did you want to see what happened as it landed?

→ Repeat with your eyes looking somewhere else in the room.

Notice how it feels – perhaps strange, as if you do not care?

→ Repeat the action with your eyes closed.

How quickly did you open your eyes to see if you had succeeded?

→ Throw the object again without any particular aim.

Notice if you cared where it landed.

AND-DO-IT

Eye-Connecting

During the next few weeks:

→ Notice when you look at people you are talking with. You may find with some types of information you do not even look at them at all!

→ Notice if your eyes trail away before your spoken thought has been completed.

→ Make a decision to keep your eyes connected **'in the zone'** with the person or people you are talking with.

→ Keep eye contact into the silence, after you have finished talking.
Does this help you see whether they have understood you? Does the necessity or pull to repeat yourself, alter?

→ Notice the eye movements of other people as they talk to/with you.

→ During an unpressurised conversation see if you can notice slight changes which may happen on the other person's face. For example, focus on their mouth and the tension of their lips.

→ Notice what happens to the way you speak when eye-contact is not possible: on the phone, driving the car, during a conference call...
For example do you interrupt others since you are less aware if they have finished what they were saying, or conversely do you leave more silence as you wait to hear if the other person has finished what they wanted to say?

6 Our Voice

This section includes three AND-DO-ITs
    ...when we stop breathing...

My father has been dead for more than 20 years. If I look at photos of him it helps me bring him to life in my memory. I also have his voice on tape, which I hardly ever dare to listen to. When I do listen to it, I get goose pimples. The sound of his voice creates a strange mixture of an incredible closeness with him as if he is standing in the room, together with a deep sadness. My father, who was Austrian, had a strong Austrian-German accent when he spoke English. I had never noticed this consciously until I listened to the tape after he had died. I was amazed. Yet I knew without a doubt that this was my father's voice. I also heard for the first time that he had a slight lisp. Even now it seems strange to me that I did not notice this when he was alive. Is voice recognition experienced predominantly on a visceral level and is that why it can potentially be so compelling?

Within your family or group of friends do you know a few people who, if you hear their voice on the phone, you instantly recognise? Or conversely they instantly recognise your voice? If so, it will probably be someone who creates a strong positive or negative emotional response in you. I enjoy being able to ring one of the few people I know that well, and not have to give my name. There is a feeling of connection, closeness and understanding when I am recognised purely by the melody of my voice. Or similarly, if I instantly recognise their voice before they say their name, the GAP closes between us. Strangely, this feeling of closeness and familiarity can also be created by the voice of someone we do not know personally, for example a public figure, famous actor or singer. Have you ever listened to the singing of a favourite artist to help you feel more at home in unfamiliar surroundings, or more relaxed when the pressures of life are mounting?

Each person's voice has a unique quality; it is their sound signature. If I think of famous speeches and speakers of the 20th century, for example Sir Winston Churchill or Martin Luther King, the unforgettable resonance of their voice also comes to mind.

If you have ever heard a recording of your voice, which will be close to how others hear you, does it feel familiar or strange? An initial reaction from many people is: *"Oh no, do I really sound like that?"* And yet from a slightly different perspective, we hear our own voice every time we talk. The production of sound in the form of what we call our voice is a direct result of the vibrations of our vocal chords in our throat and the subsequent resonating in our body. It is a technical action and reaction. Common enough information, yet beyond this basic knowledge, most of us never learn how to use the full capability of our voice. Consequently, many people use only a small amount of this potentially powerful communication tool.

Being able to talk will be an important element in almost any job, yet who considers themselves a professional talker? How many of us know or even have a desire to learn more about using the full instrument of our voice?

Vocal tensions
There are numerous physical elements that have a direct effect on the sound of the voice. During each day the body will collect and sometimes store various tensions. Here follows a basic list of some areas in the body which if tense or relaxed will affect the sound: lips, tongue, jaw, throat, neck, shoulders, arms, chest...in fact down through the whole body to the toes. I have found that even when a person's toes and feet are tense it has a negative impact on the resonance of their voice. So yes, the whole body is a sounding board. In particular the position of the chin and how we breathe make an important contribution to a full, inspiring sound.

These tensions can come from long term personal history. For example, at school you may not have been allowed to talk in class, and to prevent yourself from uttering your thoughts, you kept your mouth firmly shut with steel tight lips. This lip tension is now your norm. Alternatively it could be a tension from your last meeting when someone frustrated your actions and your jaw muscle clenched in annoyance. If you do not do something about it, both long term and short term muscle tensions will get between you and your full voice. To hear some of these effects try the following: say one word or a short sentence and then repeat it with your teeth clenched tightly together, then repeat it with your face stretched towards the ceiling and finally with your chin dropped towards your chest. You will probably hear that the quality of the sound changes.

The breath
One of the meanings of the verb 'to inspire' is to breathe in. And funnily enough the word 'expire' can mean both to breathe out as well as die. If someone has a flowing deep breath, the effect on others is usually positive, and will contribute to them being inspiring. There are many occasions when we stop breathing for a few seconds and we can even get into a habit of holding our breath. As you continue to read this section see if you can simultaneously notice the rhythm of your breathing. The held breath can happen when we are concentrating hard on something, waiting for a moment to say a thought in between other people's words in a group discussion, or when we suddenly feel frightened or surprised. It is usually a moment of tension, an action of holding ourselves in. The result is that we get less oxygen coming into our bodies. If we stop breathing for too long we lose consciousness and faint. So particularly during moments of pressure and tension it is useful to not only keep a flowing and constant breath, but also make sure that our breath is not shallow and gasping but low and deep into our lungs. A high breath (short quick breaths just using the top of our lung capacity) can not only make us feel dizzy and muddy our thinking but it also has a dramatic effect on the resonance of our voice, creating a higher pitched, thin, tight sound. There are many ways to re-find a low breath, one of which is explained at the end of this section.

It is useful to consistently re-find a low breath not only for the resonance in your voice, but also for your general well-being. Many meditation techniques place an emphasis on this way of breathing.

Vocal Patterns
All of us, as we learn to talk and then continue on into the rough and tumble of childhood, will take on a collection of vocal patterns. These patterns whether they are useful or not become habitual and sometimes, if we are not aware of them, will stay with us our whole life.

Some common vocal habits
→ The repeated speed of the sound of each word: clipped and fast, lethargic and slow...
→ The speed of one word after another in a sentence.
→ A pushing sound.
→ Persistently ending each thought with a rising or falling inflection.
→ Dipping off with the volume at the end of each thought or sentence.
→ A great or small variation on any of the previous patterns.
→ An inaudible volume.
→ An inappropriately loud volume.
→ A flat disconnected intonation.
→ An over-exuberant, artificial intonation.

These habits will often have nothing to do with the reality and need of a particular interaction, and will therefore create varying GAPs of understanding. If your habit is to talk fast and the person you are talking with is also a fast talker and listener, no problem. But is that matching always the case? How well do you get on with people who have different vocal habits from yourself?

The impact of your voice and how it is received will also be connected to where you are looking. This is fundamental for effective interactions and is described in the previous section: Eyes & Contact.

Voice and Emotions

We are continually experiencing different mixtures of emotions. This will in turn colour our vocal sound. The idea is not a particularly new one. It is beautifully described in the Dutch novel *Max Havelaar* by Multatuli (the nom de plume of Eduard Douwes Dekker) written in 1859.

> Havelaar paused for a moment. In order to have an idea of the impression his words produced, one would have had to hear and see him. When he spoke of his child there was something soft in his voice, something indescribably moving, which provoked the question: "Where is the little one? I cannot wait to kiss the child that makes his father speak like this!" But when shortly afterwards, with little apparent transition, he passed on to ask why LEBAK was poor, and why so many of its inhabitants left to go elsewhere, something in his tone reminded one of the sound of a gimlet being forcefully screwed into hard wood. And yet he did not speak loudly, nor did he put any stress on particular words [...]
>
> His metaphors and images, always taken from the life around him, really were, to him, instruments for making his meaning exactly clear to his audience, and not, as is so often the case, the irksome appendages that hinder orators without helping to illuminate the matter they profess to be explaining. We are nowadays quite accustomed to the absurd expression *as strong as a lion*. But the person who first used that simile in Europe showed that he had not drawn it from the poesy of the soul, which reasons in pictures and cannot speak otherwise, but had merely copied this commonplace image from some book or other – perhaps the Bible – in which a lion occurred. For none of his audience had ever experienced the strength of a lion; and consequently it would be more to the point to make them realise 'that' strength, by comparing it with something whose strength was known to them all from experience, than vice versa.

It is worth noting that in this passage he has identified how important the choice of imagery is to evoke authentic sound-emotion in the speaker.

Images have to come from the personal experience of the speaker. Borrowed images will resound in the melody of someone's voice as hollow and insincere. Genuine feelings will resonate in the voice whether you want this to happen or not.

When we channel the emotions through the voice it can be not only an enjoyable communication tool, but the resulting effect can be inspiring. Unfortunately, some emotions have various 'technical' side effects which provoke negative stereotype labelling. For example: if I am feeling enthusiastic, what could happen is that my voice becomes high and shrill. As I am female I may then be described as being hysterical. Another particularly female stereotype is when a woman is attempting to state a point of view in a determined way. The voice can sound hard and pushed, in which case she may easily receive the label 'bitch'. Males may be labelled as pushy, aggressive or dominating.

If you take a more passive or re-active position in a relationship, the sound of the emotions you are feeling will be evident, even if you attempt to hide them. Very often if we feel strong negative emotions they will translate into a physical tension in our throat. As the vocal chords are located in the throat, it can sometimes be so dramatic that we get literally choked and cannot even utter one word.

When talking with someone who has a warm resonating voice you may label them as being a warm and understanding person. The voice can be surprisingly comforting and reassuring, even if the content of the message is unpleasant. Similarly if someone has a brittle tight sound, they will be harder to listen to on a visceral level, regardless of how interesting the content may be.

When used well, our voices have an extraordinary range and potential to physically put others at ease, inspire and motivate. Sound waves have a real and physical effect on our bodies and our sense of discomfort or comfort. The screech of a car's brakes, the song of a bird, the push and pull of waves on a beach, a door creaking open. Recently it has been found that certain sound waves even have a healing effect on the cells in our bodies.

If someone wants to have a more proactive and skilled communication relationship then they need to learn basic vocal techniques. I would love to be able to help with this right now but I believe the voice needs a professional ear or at least personal contact. This could happen during some sessions with a singing or voice teacher. If you decide to take a few voice lessons, see if the teacher can help you with the following:

→ Locating and releasing any physical tensions you have, which prevent your voice from resonating fully.
→ Giving you some exercises to do the above so that you can discreetly check this any time, any place.
→ Some exercises to help you explore pitch and timbre.
→ Some exercises to help you free up your articulation (tongue, jaw, lips, throat).
→ Some exercises to help you feel an easy low breath and understand what part the diaphragm plays in this.

Like many things in life, if we understand and apply the technical requirements then we can have more space to successfully explore our potential and interpretation of the content. The voice is a clear example of this, and the learning curve can be compared to that of learning to play a sport or a musical instrument. If we learn how to really use our voice, this voice which carries all those important thoughts to others, it can have a massive impact on our personal effectiveness in every area of our life. And with this increase of effectiveness, since a beautiful expressive voice is such a physical and emotional experience, the level of pleasure will also increase.

AND-DO-IT

Re-Finding a Low Easy Breath

→ Lie on your back on the floor with a couple of books under your head (not too high or too low but continuing the natural curve of your spine, keeping the back of your neck long with your chin comfortably towards your chest).

→ Have your knees bent and your feet on the floor so that you use as little effort as possible to maintain your position.

→ Put your hands on your lower belly, near your hips.

→ Let your breath find its own rhythm – mouth slightly open, breathing through your mouth and nose.

→ Let the weight of your body be fully supported by the floor. Notice where your body touches the floor.

→ As you breathe in feel your belly expand.

→ As you breathe out feel your belly sink downwards.

When this happens IT IS YOUR LOW BREATH.

Many people, particularly when they stand up, develop the tendency, as they breathe in, to suck inwards with their belly and therefore reverse the above action.

AND-DO-IT
The Length and Strength of the Breath

Using a low breath try the following structure:

→ Breathe in for one count.

→ Hold for one count.

→ Breathe out for one count.

→ Hold for one count.

Repeat this sequence increasing the count by one each time until you reach ten.

When you hold your breath, the action should be from your belly and diaphragm, rather than closing off your throat or tensing your neck.

AND-DO-IT

Voice Detective

Each day during conversations with others start to notice some of their vocal habits.
Pay attention to the following qualities:

→ Speed of one word after the next.

→ Eye contact.

→ Length of the sound of each word.

→ Pitch at different times during the thoughts and emotions.

→ Tension or mobility of the jaw.

This will give you both more information about what they are thinking and help you to become increasingly aware of sound and your own vocal potential.

7 Tempo, Timing & Cross Cultural Understanding

This section includes two AND-DO-ITs
   ...To seduce yourself to want to...

In sport speed can be crucial; with racing it is the most important factor. In tennis the speed with which the player plunges for the ball or reacts to a backhand return is admired. And with today's technology the actual velocity of the ball during a serve is noted and quoted with reverence.

If we hear a musician play a certain piece with speed and dexterity, a general response will be awe and admiration. But if the interpretation is weak, the pleasure for the listener is dramatically reduced.

If someone does lots of things in a short time span others may admire them. *"How do you manage to write so many reports, text-message with such speed, answer so many phone calls, have so many meetings, read so many articles or books, make so many decisions, in so little time?"* If you can read fast, react fast, calculate fast, it is considered an asset. But is the quality also measured?

When a child understands and learns consistently quickly, this child will probably be categorised as 'smart'. Conversely if a child takes a while to understand or learn something, they may be pigeonholed as 'a bit slow', the subtext being that the child is not so bright. Early on in our lives we will be encouraged to equate speed with ability and intelligence, particularly in western cultures. In the east there seems to be more of a counterbalance in valuing slow actions. For example, to perform the Tai Chi sequence with extreme slowness, flow and control, is one of the skills and qualities most sought after, in order to master the exercise.

With fast thinkers, particularly in monoculture meetings, it is common to see people getting tempted into trying to speak at the same speed as their own multi-layered thinking. It is mission impossible.

And even if they manage to get close to spewing out those fascinating thoughts in tempo with their mind, is there any point if most of what they say zaps past everyone in the room and out the window?

We often forget to consider the speed of communication as a changing phenomenon, which can be influenced by the environment. If you are driving, the speed will certainly be determined by what kind of car you have, but what about where you are driving, and what the conditions of the road are? Are you on the motorway, in a city, a mountain pass or approaching a traffic light? Is it during the day or at night? Is the road wet, covered in black ice, ten inches of snow or completely dry? There are many factors and we quite naturally take them into consideration as we accelerate. Unless we have a death wish!

As noted, people absorb facts, concepts and situations at very different speeds. If someone is unaware of the varied thinking and speaking tempos of others, and tries to drag along a group or an individual's understanding and interaction at their innate pace, they may end up wasting everyone's time. The delivery of their content will not land; it will not be effectively received. There will be a communication pile-up or collision. And since the discovery and development of new ideas involves a spectrum of personal and interpersonal thinking, creative collaboration will also become blocked.

To be tempo-aligned in such a way that you gather up the ebb and flow of a variety of people's attention and ability to receive information, can stimulate the thinking-interaction of everyone, even if you are doing most of the talking.

How would you assess your personal tempo?

As you read this, are you trying to get to the end of the sentence, chapter, book... or are you giving yourself varied thinking rhythms, to dwell differently on the range of ideas and images? If we are overfocussed on the desire to achieve or formulate an opinion, speed can be a gripping component.

Similarly with speed-reading: it can be a useful technique, but when is it appropriate to quickly harvest surface information, rather than appreciate the multiple layers of style, innuendo, subtext? How about speed-reading a poem? I don't think so.

Strategically waiting for the best moment to say or do something can make quite an impact on the subsequent results. This may not fit in with how you are immediately feeling, so developing the self-control to be able to speed up, slow down or wait is part of the leadership package.

To notice when it is best to inspire others to join our speed, and when to adjust to theirs, will in its very action help create dynamic relationships.

Relationship

Relation................ Ship

Ship the relating towards each other
MAKE A RELATING

Better late than ships passing in the night.

Re-late

Be on time with your lateness

A state of shipment
A ship meant for you and we.

As we work in an increasingly multi-cultural world, social gatherings and meetings in the workplace often have a cross cultural mix of participants. To identify the barriers which prevent one culture understanding another, we can start with something as basic as the tempo of the spoken word. This tempo will have a direct correlation with the success of cross cultural leadership. An ongoing frustration which people come up against, is having to speak and do business in a language other than their mother tongue. They will regularly experience a dislocation between the sophistication of their thinking, and that of their talking in, for example, English. When the majority of people in a meeting are more at ease with the English language than one or two of the group members, it can lead to the 'foreigners' not being fast enough to jump in with a thought or opinion. This can build up; they become less and less verbally active. The result is an ever-increasing GAP between them and everyone else, the meeting loses their input and the intellectual capital of the company is reduced. In most business gatherings it is in everyone's best interests that each person has the space and ability to contribute.

It is not only frustrating for the person who is having to compromise the speed of their thinking with their language skills, but it can also be annoying for the native speakers to slow down the conversation, to accommodate and include the diversity of the whole group. In such situations it is useful for everyone involved to develop patience. Unfortunately trying to increase patience can in itself create even more irritation – it feels like putting on the mental brakes. However, if we guide the speed of interaction by keeping the idea of **seduction** in mind, it becomes more fun and effective. **To seduce yourself to want to slow down**, draw out the words, take a moment to choose the best adjective, taste the thought, see if you are being understood before perhaps repeating. Similarly, speeding up the tempo can change an interaction away from default mode. **To seduce others** to get off their own thought train and enjoy contemplating, thinking, bending around and responding to the tempo of your input can become not only pleasurable but also inspiring.

If you approach the change of your speaking-speed with curiosity, noticing what is happening on more levels than just your personal desires and innate tempo, then the strategy of patience becomes fascinating and rewarding.

AND-DO-IT

Changing Speed – in the Talk

→ When you are not in a pressured situation, say something at a different speed to the tempo you feel most at ease with. Explore and try out in different interactions.

In this way you will not be able to glide along on cruise control. You will have to be more alert.

→ During a conversation, deliberately vary the speed when responding.

Others (particularly if you know each other) will have to be more alert with you, as they cannot, either consciously or subconsciously, predict your thinking pattern.

→ Imitate the speaking speed of others, and then deliberately talk either faster or slower than them.

Notice if the level of mutual understanding changes.

AND-DO-IT

Changing Speed – in the Walk or the Bite

→ During different moments when you are walking, deliberately walk either faster or slower than your normal speed.

Notice the change in how you feel when you vary the speed of your walking, or even looking at something.

→ Choose a few times when you are eating to vary the speed that you chew, swallow and take the next mouthful.

Notice the change of taste and sensation inside your mouth.

8 Silence

This section contains two AND-DO-ITs

...errr...ummm...like...sort of...

The silence of the graveyard...the silence of dawn...
Does silence exist? Is it what happens when no-one is talking?
When everyone stops talking is there silence?
No, there are constantly sounds both inside and around us: close by, far away.
When do we notice we are hearing them?
When do we interact with them?

And then there is another particularly noisy and often bothersome sound, the abstract chatter-sound of our thoughts. These thoughts can create a feeling of very real sounds. It could even be happening in the tone-memory of someone from your past. For example: that voice could be the negative tone-memory of someone who hurt you with his or her criticism. Or it may be the positive tone-memory of someone who supported and encouraged you.

Noisy negative thoughts often come in the form of questions:
"What do they think of me?"
"What do I think of them?"
"What is the best answer?"
"Perhaps I should...?"
"What will happen if...?"
"And did I remember to...?"

In our minds there are plenty of noises being received, both actual and imagined, and this incessant lack of silence can be continued into our speaking patterns. What often happens in conversations is that people fill any possible silence or pause with words which have no added meaning. This can be called a repetitive 'stop word', for example: *"you know what I mean?"* ... *"errr"*... *"ummm"*... *"like"*... *"sort of"* ... The effect on the listener/receiver is that they are not given any space or time to digest the ideas. And as the stop-words have no meaning and therefore do not contribute to the contents, the listener will continually have to edit the stop-word. What can also happen as the listener edits, is that some of the important information gets edited along with the stop-words. If the audience happens to be a group of schoolchildren or college students, they may stop listening to the contents altogether and start counting the number of times the teacher, lecturer or visiting 'professional' says "Ummm..." or "Actually", in the space of say 30 minutes. And then as the fun continues, make a mathematical calculation of the "Ummm" factor for the rest of the speaker's projected span of life!

What can 'taking silence' give you, your audience, colleagues, friends or family? If you pause for a moment with a feeling of commitment, it can give more weight to what you have just said. If you can hold **silence with curiosity** you may not only circumvent any feelings of self consciousness but you will also have more time to see things that generally pass you by. The additional information can have an impact on what you then choose to say. This sends the message that you notice and care if others have received your information, that you value them.

It can also give others the space to receive and reflect on what you have just said. This may increase engagement, stimulating them to ask questions which either add to, or challenge your thinking. Overall this kind of silence can create a more interactive communication.

When discussing this subject someone will often interject with the frustration: *"All well and good, but in most of my meetings if I stop talking for a few seconds, then other people do not necessarily ask worthwhile questions, but rather they jump in and take over."* So part of this is not only how to stop talking yourself and give others space to reflect, but also how to sustain moments of silence in a meeting or conversation and then, if you wish to, continue speaking yourself.

In the performing arts we call this 'holding the silence'. If you have ever been to a classical concert you will have experienced that moment of stillness just before the music starts, as the conductor holds their arms in the air; the orchestra sits poised to play and the audience stops coughing. It is achieved with a combination of social and cultural rules balanced with people's desires and expectations. This stillness and focussed silence may also be experienced just before the athlete jumps, or the chess player makes their next move.

Once you have 'held the silence', at a certain moment you will then need to let it go. There is no formula for the timing of this, it will all come down to what you sense, observe and are willing to play with. If we return to the conductor image, at the end of the concert they will hold their arms in the air after the orchestra plays the last note, letting the final musical moment extend and settle into the silence of the auditorium. Then with an intuitive clear action the conductor brings their arms down and the audience will (usually) understand the sign and start to clap.

During conversations, meetings and speeches, we can develop various subtle signs to indicate when are the best moments for others to talk. The skill of holding silence will come through a combination of the way you hold you body, use your gestures, sustain your eye contact, project your voice and use the physical space around you. As a general rule it is created through maintaining a few moments of stillness, directly after a physical or vocal action. The silence will be given to you if you focus this sustained attention out towards everyone.

We can also 'conduct' or lead the silence from the point of view of being a listener. To be able to listen and consider what is being said, without immediately adding extra thoughts, will give others the space to develop their thinking. Sometimes a nod or a smile in silence can be more profound and inspiring than a string of additional words.

Moments of silence can add a sense of value to your contents and to everyone involved in the conversation.

It will support the feeling of talking **with** rather than **at** each other.

A deeper understanding of the use and even power of silence will come directly through experiencing and exploring 'holding the silence'.

AND-DO-IT
Sound-Layer Listening

→ Listen to the variety of sounds you can hear.

→ Identify and count them.

→ Notice the different distances of their possible origins.

→ Can you spend a few minutes listening, hearing and following all the sounds together as one whole?

→ If you have not already done this, now consider the sounds inside yourself. If your stomach is not rumbling then there will certainly be the sounds of swallowing and breathing.

→ Listen.

AND-DO-IT
Elastic Silence

Focus on the following ideas during meetings and conversations.

Using sustained eye contact and an energised physical presence:

→ Wait a beat before answering someone's question.

→ Wait a beat between thinking one thought and the next.

→ Wait a couple of beats between one spoken thought and the next.

→ Once you become more comfortable with short silences, extend and vary the length of time.

9 Giving & Receiving

This section includes two AND-DO-ITs
   ...If the chocolates fall...

We are giving and receiving information continually, even when we sleep. It will be a variation of information to and from other people, an interaction with our different environments and an interaction with our thoughts and feelings. The exchanges are all too often automatic. This endless stimulation can range from exciting to tiring and even annoying. So how, when and why do we choose or prioritise which piece of stimulation to be aware of, learn from or respond to?

If you are trying to concentrate on writing an email or report and there is the constant chatter of someone on the telephone in your vicinity, for many it can be hard to shut out the sound intrusion. However, some people have a great capacity to not hear the sounds around them when they are focussing their thinking on something specific. My father could completely shut off from the chatter of others when he was absorbed in his own thoughts. This worked well for him if he needed to think clearly about something, but it could be surprisingly frustrating for those around him who might need a reply to a simple question. In some situations this form of concentration can be useful, and if it does not come naturally to you, then it can be trained by developing levels of awareness. Unwanted sound, sometimes called sound pollution, can lead people to extreme reactions of frustration and annoyance, even to the point of violence. Who of us has not at some time tried to shut out the cacophony of someone else's music, party-making or DIY in a vain attempt to relax or even sleep?

Different countries also have different thresholds of acceptable sound/volume interaction. For example, the difference of sound stimulation if I walk down the street in Amsterdam (the Netherlands) or in Mumbai (India) is massive. For me, a European, it can take some time to get used to the sound-colour of the East. Whereas some people, whatever their cultural background, may welcome the sounds of others as a means for them to drown out their incessant internal conversations. But sound pollution, particularly in cities, can regularly prevent effective giving and receiving of information. A familiar example is when the acoustics in a restaurant are so bad that to maintain a conversation during the meal is a struggle between asking your colleague or friend to repeat themselves, upping your own volume and bluffing having heard what the other person has just said.

With visual stimulation it is easier to interrupt, we can simply close our eyes and we no longer see. However, this is not possible if, for example, we are driving. Smell, well we could hold our nose for a short time but we cannot survive without breathing for long, and touch and taste are continuous. Interestingly, I find it almost impossible to experience a simultaneous and equal appreciation of the five senses. Try it.

We often experience the senses in a hierarchical pattern according to our individual development and abilities. For example, if I go to a performance of contemporary dance with my partner, as I have spent many years painting and drawing I will easily be pulled towards focussing on the visuals and not the music, whereas he is a professional musician so it is impossible for him to disregard the music.

Or we are pulled by whichever sense is dominating the other senses due to the circumstances. As we bite into a delicious mouthful of food it will probably be taste; standing on a mountain top looking across the valley, sight; breathing in the scent of a flower, smell; hearing the voice of a dear friend, sound; or feeling the comforting warm water of a morning shower, touch. This interactive stimulation of our senses will keep changing as the quantity and quality varies. In an attempt to focus our thinking it is common to spend a lot of each day, shutting out unwanted so-called 'background' stimulation. Not only from sound but from all of the five senses. This habitual dimming of the sensitivity of our senses can mean we remain numbed out even after the need to concentrate and focus has long passed. Are we throwing the baby out with the bathwater?

As noted, a shutting out mechanism can be useful if we wish to focus our minds on a specific thing, as in the case of my father. But either shutting out or letting in external stimulation can have a direct effect on the quality of information which is perceived and exchanged. What I mean here by quality is three-fold: how much of any intended information do you actually receive, how much do you need to receive, and thirdly does it feed you? Similarly how accurate and effective is the information you are giving to others, how much do they really need and do they also feel nourished? Please note that at this point I am not looking at agreement or disagreement on the content, but simply understanding and receiving another's information or idea.

In the case of a gift, for example a box of chocolates, the exchange of information will have a physical actuality. The giving goes with the physical action of passing the chocolates from one pair of hands (the giver) to the other pair of hands (the receiver). The action will have some kind of conclusion as the receiver (usually) expresses thanks. If the chocolates fall on the floor during the exchange it is also obvious that there has been a disturbance in the intended action, and most probably either one or both parties will pick up the chocolates. As far as effectively giving information to other people is concerned, we are often more careless than we would be with the box of chocolates in observing if it has been received.

With an over-stimulated, often racing mind the receiver may also not be so clear with the messages they project whilst receiving. For example, if we look specifically at the giving and receiving of a compliment, nine times out of ten the receiver of the compliment immediately starts analysing what they think of the compliment and whether they agree, rather than first receiving it and responding with a simple *"thank you"*. This may happen because they feel shy or unused to being praised and as a defence mechanism try and justify themselves, for example:

"Hey you look really relaxed today" --- *"Oh do I, well I slept longer than usual last night"*

"I read your report, it's very clear" --- *"I hope so, I worked for hours on it"*

"This meal is delicious" --- *"It is such an easy recipe, I have cooked it a thousand times.'*

This way of trying to rationalise a compliment rather than simply accepting it, is sometimes used as a way to not appear arrogant. Funnily enough this tactic can even create an effect of arrogance.

People also muddle up the action of receiving information, by saying thank you, with the action of agreeing to, or even giving the impression we understand the comment. How can you try the chocolate if you do not first take it into your own hands? It is only after you have received the chocolate that you can actually bite into it, taste it and then decide if you like it or not.

So the *'thank you'* or similar words of marking receipt are solely an initial acknowledgement and appreciation of the act of giving. It does not mean agreement or even understanding.

One of the tiring and inefficient side effects of omitting to acknowledge receipt in the form of some kind of *'thank you,'* can be that the giver does not feel their comment has been received. They then become compelled to repeat it. AND THEY DO. This type of interaction can contribute to endless re-stating of information and therefore create unnecessarily long meetings. The pattern also occurs in families where familiarity seduces us into feeling we do not have to acknowledge each other's questions or statements. It can then quite easily escalate into irritation and even arguments, with the exasperated parent or partner exclaiming: *"I have asked you four times to come to the dinner table, please react...come NOW,"* or the child complaining:

"You never listen to me…" Can you recall how frustrating and even lonely it can feel if others are not listening to or valuing your opinion or request?

The positive effect of giving a clear message when receiving a piece of information is that the interaction becomes more efficient and compact. When the other person feels that the information has 'landed' they are less likely to repeat themselves.

Different cultures have quite a variety of codes regarding receiving from each other. For example in the UK, saying please and thank you can become almost compulsive. Conversely, people in Holland will often have a more informal approach to this etiquette. When I was a newcomer to Holland I questioned if I was overdoing the way I encouraged my seven-year-old (Dutch) stepson to say, *"thank you"*. It was then pointed out to me that the act of thanking is an acknowledgement and respect of their separateness. It helps define the line where one person's ego stops and another person's ego begins. As each country culture or corporate culture has its own subtle ways of expressing the *"thank you"* it is useful to be informed and choose accordingly. In addition to the formal please and thank you etiquette, we have a variety of ways to indicate or acknowledge receiving someone's thoughts, for example with a nod of the head the same important definition is made.

A simple word or movement marking the action of receiving creates respect and exchange, and individuality will be defined.

The other person whom we often do not clearly give to, is ourselves. Do we take enough moments between receiving and analysing, and also give ourselves space to consider and develop our ideas? Simply put, after you have given an initial word or sign of receiving another person's opinion, you can pause for thought, rather than rushing on to say the first reply/idea which comes into your mind.

With this purposefully taken moment, you give yourself time to choose and strategise a response. This is particularly useful if you hold a leadership position with complex responsibilities, where your choice of how to reply to any remark may be crucial.

AND-DO-IT
The Simple "Thank You"

When someone gives you a compliment, try just sincerely saying "thank you."

It is important that the receiver looks into the eyes of the compliment giver and holds this contact for a moment.

AND-DO-IT
Time Saver

→ Each time someone gives you either a compliment or just information **resist immediately having or giving an opinion**. First give a clear acknowledgement of receipt vocally and/or physically. Make sure you maintain eye contact. This does not mean you agree with the point of view, it means you have received it and you are clearly showing this.

→ Then as a separate second action take a moment to see what you think about it.

→ The third action is to respond, maybe with your point of view. Or as my daughter when she was younger once said:
"point of you."

→ Notice that the other person is less likely to repeat their idea in its initial form when they sense you have received it.

The more you can separate the moment of receiving information from your response to what you actually feel or think about it, the shorter meetings will become. This is mostly due to the reduction of restated information.

Even in heated discussions, the more that you can make the above difference between the receiving and the evaluating of information, the more the exchange can develop and move on rather than go round and round in circles.

Note the difference between saying:
"Yes but ..." (Negating)
or
"Yes and ..." (Receiving and adding)

10 Levels of Listening Distracted Versus Focussed

This section has one AND-DO-IT

...relatively small passive-aggressive actions...

If in a meeting or conference we are required to say nothing and just listen, we may feel unable to have an influence over the quality of the interaction. We may even feel it is a waste of our time to only listen and seemingly not be able to join in the discourse. I have noticed that this is more likely to be a listener's reaction if they are used to taking the lead, or if the people who are talking are not engaging speakers. If we feel frustrated, bored or distracted it is easy to stop listening. So if the aim of the meeting is to exchange information and become more informed, then the consequences of 'zoning out' will be that both the speaker and the listener are indeed throwing their time away.

Not only will the listener be wasting their time, but other people can easily be affected by their lack of interest. Each one of us can have quite an influence on the rest of the group. Have you ever sat next to someone who is actively showing disinterest? This is often conveyed by quite small actions, such as tapping a foot, doodling, making little side comments, slumping back in the chair, staring out of the window (as noted in the section: Eyes & Contact), checking phone messages and emails. You may be irritated or distracted by them, you may collude and sometimes that person may even be you.

Whilst spending time or working with groups of people, you will probably have experienced how dominant one negative or distracted person can be, even if that negativity is only displayed in relatively small passive-aggressive actions, as noted above. If someone is showing disinterest, the speaker may not feel their information is really being received, with the consequence that they repeat and repeat. The agony is prolonged.

It can be underestimated how much each one of us can learn from simply listening well. Recently it was discovered that by watching and listening to others, we learn on more than just a cognitive level. In the early 1990s, at the University of Parma, Italy, research professors including Leonardo Fogassi, Vittorio Gallese and Giacomo Rizzolatti showed how some monkeys perceive and imitate – as in the saying, 'Monkey see, monkey do.' The Parma group observed that when a macaque monkey saw another monkey or even person perform a specific action, such as picking up an object, the same neurons fired in its brain as when it performed that action itself. They called these 'mirror neurons'. Their later work showed humans have a 'mirror neuron' system as well, which could explain how we also learn by seeing and feeling each other's emotions and intentions. If a speaker is actively engaged in re-imagining their ideas as they explain their thinking, then the attentive listener's 'mirror neurons' will emulate the speaker's experience and understanding will occur on several different levels.

In addition, it appears that when a person mentally rehearses a speech or action, the same neurons are activated as if they have actually uttered those words or made that physical action. This idea is being used in the professional sports world whereby top athletes have a mental as well as a physical coach. It has been shown that if we interchange rehearsing actual action with rehearsing the same movement in our imagination, it increases our excellence. The 'action' in the brain is almost the same as performing it, except that the actual implementation in our muscles is somehow blocked.

'Mirror neurons' appear to be essential to the way we learn. Imitative learning has long been recognised as a major component of childhood development. And finding out about 'mirror neurons' could explain how we can also increase our ability to do something by simply watching. Furthermore, it explains why it often feels exhilarating to watch, for example, a tennis match, football match or dance performance, as our nervous system is in part firing off as if we were performing the action ourselves.

When your role in a meeting or conference requires that you only listen, if you remain attentive and receptive, you will experience, learn and understand on more levels than you may realise.

Please note that there are many texts to be found about 'active listening'. These include such techniques as repeating what you have just heard back to the speaker in a condensed form to clarify understanding. However, what this section is referring to is the learning and understanding, which happens to you on a deeper level in your nervous system as well as on an intellectual level, when you keep alert and focussed with the person who is talking.

AND-DO-IT

Listen-Learning

→ If/when you have a predominantly listening/watching role in a meeting, make sure you are keeping your attention focussed on the person who is speaking.

→ Pro-actively give little responses to the information with a slight nod, reactive change of facial expression, eye contact or an energised sitting position.

→ Change your emotional engagement – listen from different emotional points of view.
(explained in No Man's Land section: Strategic Emotion)

This will have a win, win effect:

If the speaker sees the reactions of the audience they will be subliminally encouraged to proceed rather than get pulled into unnecessary repetition.

You will effectively absorb relevant information and learn from the speaker's experience, it will feed you on more levels than you may initially realise.

11 Crying in Public

This section contains one AND-DO-IT
…Oh, you are being emotional again…

Why is it often hard to know what to do when someone cries? Why do we sometimes feel compelled to try and stop them, or on the contrary find it a relief? And if you are the person with the tears, what prevents you from letting the emotion run its course?

Crying is clearly one of the ways we release built up emotional tensions, often related to fear, anger, grief, pain, frustration and disappointment. Some cry-triggers can come from us empathising with another person's distress. The list of cry-emotions quickly gravitates towards the negative ones, although with abandoned laughter I can also have tears streaming down my face. We cry for a wide range of reasons, and it can also have a wide range of effects on others.

The display of crying will also have cultural and gender codes connected to it. However, the newborn baby will cry with abandon, without taking its cultural heritage or gender into consideration. From our first baby moments, crying is one of our main tools to alert the adults around us to our needs, desires and possible frustrations. As we develop and acquire other skills and survival tools, for example language and muscle control, we refine the way we use our tears. The way we develop our ability or lack of ability to cry as an adult, will have been strongly influenced by the reactions of the important people around us as we grew up.

With words and/or actions we may be encouraged to cry:
"It is OK, I am here…"
"This pain you are feeling is awful, you poor darling…"
"I understand your frustrations, take all the time you need…"
"I am so sorry to hear this is happening to you…"

And/or you receive:
- → a sympathetic hug with no urgency from them to stop you crying.
- → a warm shoulder to lean on.
- → compassionate sustained eye contact.

Or discouraged to cry:
"Be strong, don't cry."
"Oh, you are being emotional again."
"Please stop crying, I have done everything I can to help. It is not my fault."
"Oh no, why are you crying? Are you OK? I am so worried about you."
And/or you receive:
- → an impatient hug or hurried patting with the aim to stop you crying as fast as possible.
- → an embarrassed looking away.
- → or the person finds an excuse to leave the room.

Take a moment to note which of the above quotes resonates with you.

If our tears regularly create a negative response in others in the form of impatience, embarrassment or even fear this will probably inhibit our ease with crying. Similarly, the way our tears were received by others when we were a child, will also influence the level of ease we may feel when confronted with another's tears as an adult.

We all need to learn to control our tears for different reasons. If we do not develop this skill, an adult interaction would proceed quite differently than the accepted norm. Can you imagine how an adult dinner party might develop if each minor disappointment was met with a gush of tears? Funnily enough just thinking about that kind of dramatic possibility makes me want to laugh. Television sit-coms regularly use exaggerated tears as a theatrical tool to provoke laughter.

But in day-to-day life, why, both as the person crying, and as the person witnessing crying, can we feel uncomfortable? Why are we so clumsy when we interact with this emotion, particularly when we are in a professional situation? In the West many child-females are allowed to cry as they grow up, and many child-males are regarded as weak and un-male if even their bottom lip starts to quiver with emotion. Such dissimilar reactions create two quite different habits with crying. The most frequent behaviour pattern I have come across, is when experiencing high emotion, many women cry, whilst men are more likely to numb out, shout or throw something. Whilst the person who has shouted or thrown something may retrospectively feel like a bit of an idiot, as they lost control of their temper, I doubt if they would feel humiliated or weak. But often there seems to be something feeble and shameful about crying.

Many times in discussions with female professionals, they describe workplace situations where they felt so strongly about something, that at the time it triggered a cry reaction in them. This then had a variety of consequences:

→ They leave the room as quickly as possible so as not to be seen to cry.
→ They choke back the tears and do not dare talk for the rest of the meeting, in case they fail to stifle their feelings.
→ They are unable to suppress the tears, apologise and are met with such comments from their (often male) colleagues as: *"You are being too emotional..." "Let's talk about this later when you have calmed down..." "Your emotions are getting the better of you, you obviously cannot cope with the pressure..." "I am sorry you are upset, it is making me feel very uncomfortable..."*

I was recently talking at a conference where yet again a young female executive came up to me and related how that same morning her boss had sent her out of a meeting, as she had had slightly wet eyes during a heated discussion. His reason: she was being too emotional. This thirty-six-year-old woman felt like a little child being reprimanded by her headmaster. Conversely, male executives regularly ask what they should do, or how they should react when faced with crying (often female) co-workers. These men describe how they feel seriously disempowered, uncomfortable and even personally responsible.

The way someone cries, as well as the way we react to someone crying, can greatly influence the negative or positive effect of the tears.

So how, if we need to, can we cry without feeling ashamed, or support a crying friend or colleague without feeling embarrassed, uncomfortable or even manipulated?

Let's start with the person who is stimulated to cry.

There are the situations when someone cries due to grief, for example on hearing of the death of a loved one, a fatal illness, a shocking accident, or relief, for example at unexpected good news. In a private context we will probably not only expect that person to cry, but it will even feel strange if they do not. We know that at some point the tears will and should come. In the business context the degree of ease the person will have in being able to cry, will depend on their relationship to the other people in the group, particularly with regard to power and position. However, it will usually be acceptable for the meeting to be adjourned, or for the individual to leave, possibly with a colleague accompanying them as a support. If the person who is crying is visibly crushed by their emotion it may also stimulate empathetic tears in others. The crying which is provoked by someone else's pain or tragedy can also happen when we watch a film, read a book, look at the news on television, see a theatre piece. We will probably be drawn to cry in public as the information re-stimulates and rhymes with our personal history.

Crying can be trickier when it is triggered by frustration or passion. I believe that the key element which makes it uncomfortable for others is when the crying person is uncomfortable themselves, and so apologises for it, trying to stop the tears, rather than saying with no apology something like: *"Yes I am crying, for good reason, I feel very strongly about ..."*

If the 'crier' continues like this and lets the tears run their course it will probably not prevent them from being able to talk, and it will be absolutely clear to everyone how important the issue is for them. The possible fear of hysteria which may be running with some of the other people in the room, can be averted as they see the crying person is able to look at them without shame, talk in a clear intelligent way and at the same time have tears streaming down their face. The effect can certainly be confrontational, but it can lead to the group having a deeper understanding and respect of the crying person's point of view. This can in turn produce a more solid commitment in everyone.

It is useful for those who are not crying to privately notice if they feel discomfort with the other person's tears, and consider that it will probably rhyme with their own relationship and history with crying. This can easily cloud their ability to hear the content of what a crying person is actually saying. The next step is to make sure that anything the listener then says, even if it acknowledges the crying person's high emotion, does not judge nor attempt to stop the tears.

If we develop the skills to navigate the cry interaction in this way then each person can communicate through a full range of emotions and need not numb out in order to fit into a social or corporate culture.

The 'Cry' subject regularly comes up during personal development sessions. Since we are often identifying core emotions and behavioural habits, one of the individuals may even cry themselves. It could be the person who wears their heart on their sleeve or the person who subsequently says: *"I have not cried in years."* The latter may initially be surprised and shocked, but this soon turns into relief as years of pent-up emotions are released. It is all too often, **but not always**, gender based. Recently, a male director asked: *"Last year I was unexpectedly promoted. Before I left my old job I gave a farewell drink for my fantastic team after five years' collaboration. During the speeches I almost started crying, would that have been OK?"* The question made me wonder how many people are regularly de-humanising themselves in the public arena, by the tacit agreement that crying is weak and unprofessional. Think about how emotionally disconnected, even cold-hearted, some corporate or national leaders can be whilst discussing appalling situations. It makes one wonder about the quality of decisions which are reached in such cases.

Crying is a powerful display of core emotions. If the occasion arises when you are taking a position of authority, to be able to show that very human side of yourself in public with no apology can be inspiring. It will not only increase the sensitivity of decision making but also create a deeper group understanding and respect.

AND-DO-IT
Salting the Tears

Make a mental list of when and how often you may be moved to tears on a yearly basis.

Think back to the last time you cried in public – what was the reaction?

Think back to the last time you were with someone who was crying – what was your reaction?

If sometimes during a public interaction you are moved to tears, next time this happens:

1. Keep breathing. Move your toes and ankles, bringing your energy down into your feet.
2. Do not apologise, explain or dismiss yourself.
3. **Keep looking out towards the person/people you are talking with and see them.**
4. Keep on talking, say what you wish to say and also let the crying take its natural course.

If you are a person who when faced with someone crying feels uncomfortable and drawn to trying to stop them:

1. Keep looking at them, certainly be empathetic, but without trying to stop their tears either with words or gestures.
2. Continue the discourse, focussing your thoughts and emotions on respecting them as a strong and sensitive individual.
3. Try to put any personal discomfort you may be feeling on the pause button.

12 The Power of Laughter

This section includes one AND-DO-IT

...I am OK... we are OK... are you OK...

Colen and laughter story

During an improvisation class a group of students were each commissioned to tell a story in a specific style. Colen's assignment was to make everyone laugh. He came into the large drama studio where about twenty students were waiting. He proceeded to gather them around him, and give a rather banal description of a certain event. However, he told the story laughing, laughing so much that he could hardly get the words out. Within seconds everyone in the room was laughing too. This unforgettable knock-on effect surprised everyone. It was clear that it was not what he said but how he said it. His genuine laughter, which was stimulated by an unconnected private thought, was infectious. And for a few moments everyone was linked together through catching his laughter.

In more than twenty-five years living in Holland I have found that the majority of Dutch people have a remarkable capacity for speaking different languages, English often being one of them. This can be very tempting for an English-speaking foreigner, as they can instantly communicate without spending too much time learning Dutch. In any social situation, even if you are the only foreigner many Dutch people will quite happily speak English, for a while. Partly due to this, my ability to speak Dutch progressed slowly. The GAP became larger and larger as I regularly felt quite isolated. Then one day during a dinner with a group of Dutch friends I told a joke (in English). This created an immediate laughter response from everyone and for a moment I not only felt included, but I actually was. The whole group was connected. Over the years, I not only developed the ability to tell a joke with effective dramatic timing, but I also gathered a large repertoire of jokes to choose from as the opportunity arose. This was not a deliberate strategy, but a skill which gradually evolved, and it helped me to feel integrated.

The evolutionary origins of laughter have been traced back to about four million years ago, at which time, it is speculated, the laugh was more like a staccato panting in response to touches and tickles. Then about two million years ago our ancestors gained the ability to control their facial muscles so that they could laugh at will, as well as spontaneously. Only later, when humans evolved higher cognition and language, was laughter connected with humour.

If laughter can be divorced from humour then its primary function was social control and group communication. The ability to make someone laugh is often associated with power dynamics.

Making someone laugh puts you in a dominant position, as does laughing at someone. It has been found that women laugh more often than men, who are more likely to be the ones provoking the laughter. However, it seems that we all mostly laugh during ordinary conversation rather than as a response to jokes. Laughter is contagious – sitcom producers have used canned laughter since the 1950s for just that reason – but gelotologists (laughter experts) have yet to figure out exactly why. It could be the result of a feedback loop triggered in the brain.

The female laugh
I have noticed it is common for women to use a specific kind of 'short-giggle-laugh' to create a feeling of connection, warmth and reassurance with other people. In the workplace, it is particularly evident within all-female groups. They will probably use a lot of this affirmative 'short-giggle-laugh', carrying the sub-text: *"I am OK... we are OK... are you OK?"* This may intensify after someone makes a strong statement or takes a clear brave action. Although this little laugh can reinforce an empathetic atmosphere, it can also have a self-effacing effect, undermining the strength and clarity of a statement or action. If for example I express an opinion in a strong voice and then immediately follow it with a slight giggle, it gives a confusing signal of non-

commitment. The result can be that people do not take me seriously enough, and over time my self-confidence may be eroded. In a very competitive environment, in order to try and reassure myself, I may giggle even more after stating my opinion. It can become harder and harder to make a strong statement, and in less secure surroundings I may avoid them altogether.

Recently I was watching a panel of six professional women on television discussing social and political ideas. The small affirmative laughter and giggling was constant. A panel of males in a similar situation will tend to use laughter quite differently; if they do laugh it is often in response to something they perceive as specifically funny, rather than in an attempt to bond and feel more secure.

Using laughter well

Many of us on some level will be aware that if we can make others laugh, it can create a sense of connection and even control. However, comedy is one of the hardest forms of theatre. Worldwide there are few memorable comedians. If you have followed any successful stand-up comics you may notice how the individuals are usually very skilled in the way they use their bodies, particularly their faces, together with vocal melody, timing and the use of silence. These are the major components in creating the laughter response, it will not necessarily be hanging on the content. How often does a joke fall flat in a business context? How often does someone by trying to put both themselves and the group at ease, end up creating an embarrassing moment with that little joke-comment? We all will have different responses to what we perceive as funny, particularly in cross cultural settings. To deliver a well-timed and appropriate joke is an art, and the larger the audience the higher the odds against it succeeding.

Letting laughter come through the build-up of a story and interaction with other people can be more reliable than a planned ironic comment or joke.

Interestingly, the role of the comedian has until recently tended to be a male preserve, possibly because as a comedian you need to be prepared to make a fool of everyone, including yourself. Increasingly females are able to publicly express a fuller range of emotions, showing their 'darker' as well as their more political sides, and playing with sexuality, rather than being hampered by a need to be sexually attractive. These women are finding their own form of humour from a female perspective. This is resulting in witty and controversial shows such as the British comedy, 'Absolutely Fabulous', written by and starring Jennifer Saunders and Joanna Lumley. And in America, for example, the stand-up comedienne Sarah Silverman has hit the news headlines with her blue comedy, gallows humour and political satire.

Laughter as protection or avoidance
During group personal development programmes I regularly see participants who love to make jokes and who are often genuinely funny. These individuals are popular group members, as the laughter can cut through tensions and potentially vulnerable or confrontational moments. It creates a 'feel-good factor'. Unfortunately this very same joker, in their desire to defuse tension, will often use their wit to avoid personal engagement in the process. Depending on how chronic it is, the joking can also stop other people from exploring their own, as well as the group's potential. It is a tricky one to address. If you do not run with the joke, and question it or even bring in the idea that the joke is being used as a tool of avoidance, you may be seen as a killjoy by everyone. It is amazing how protective a group can be towards their in-house comedian. However, once the group realises what is happening they will begin to tire of, or even challenge the joker themselves. Strangely enough this can also be a relief for the joker, as they no longer feel responsible for the constant well-being of the group. If they agree to give up their power base in this area and use their talent for creating laughter with well-placed humour, everyone gains.

Laughter as a weapon

There is a big difference between laughing **at** or **with** someone. If people laugh at someone, it can range from light-hearted bravado to being surprisingly cruel. We see an extreme form of this where prisoners are humiliated by their prison warders, using the tool of laughter to ridicule them. And who of us has not experienced in the playground as a child either being laughed at by others or perhaps even doing it ourselves? Bullying has a very particular kind of laughter connected to it. The effect will be that the GAP closes between the group of people laughing and widens between them and the person who is being laughed at. Of course if it is light-hearted, and the individual also has the ability to laugh at themselves, then a deeper level of mutual appreciation may result. However, it takes a self-confident and mature personality to be able to laugh at themselves. Perhaps the idea in the line: *"Life is far too important to be taken seriously"*, from Irish dramatist, poet, and author Oscar Wilde can help us to lighten up?

AND-DO-IT
Behind the Laughter

Over the next weeks notice:

→ The female 'reassuring' laugh.

→ The person who has a gift for humour.

→ The joke that succeeds.

→ The joke that falls flat.

→ Group laughter.

Is the laugh used to entertain, release tension, create a bond, create avoidance, include or exclude others?

13 The Smile Confusion

This section includes two AND-DO-ITs
...he is a heartless bastard...

What is true for the complexity of laughter is also true for the smile. The subtlety of a smile can give a variety of messages, from a positive sign of welcoming appreciation, to that of distance and negative criticism. The smile is our first physical expression towards laughter. The smile is an amazing tool to open the communication door between both friends and strangers, and it is frequently received as an invitation to connect, close the GAP. If you smile at someone they will probably smile back, and in this way a dialogue begins. A smile can have different meanings in different countries, so if you are travelling to or doing business with a culture which is very different from your experience to date, it can be helpful to do a bit of research on this subject. However, the kind of smiles which in many cultures give a fairly simple message include the smiles of generosity, happiness, victory, satisfaction, seduction, shyness and empathy.

Apart from specific cultural codes, which you may or may not know about, the following types of smiles regularly create a GAP in understanding.

In general if your smile is a frozen habitual facial expression, people may perceive you as distant, insincere, phoney or arrogant. Some people develop the frozen smile as a way to survive an unpleasant past experience, and it becomes their permanent 'at rest' facial expression. And some people habitually smile as they say one thing, whilst thinking another. It is almost impossible to know this about yourself unless someone points it out.

Then there is the cover-up-smile of: *"I know...but I am not going to tell you..."* It can happen when a person decides not to speak their mind. For example, they are feeling frustrated or annoyed but believe their opinion will not be considered or taken seriously so they say nothing.

In which case the smile easily turns into a grimace. Conversely, a person may hold back in telling something for fun or suspense. And then, as in the case of Leonardo da Vinci's Mona Lisa, it can have an enigmatic effect.

There is also the forced smile, when you do not actually feel like smiling but you do it as you think you ought to. This will probably come over as stressed and artificial. The effect on others can be one of disbelief or mistrust.

Another out of place smile which I regularly see, is when someone feels embarrassed, shy or uncomfortable. The person may be describing something sad or unpleasant, with a big smile on their face. They are having an overpowering emotion and, in their attempt to cope with this in a public context, they subconsciously resort to a smile to dilute or hide the real feeling.

For example: Mr Boz has to tell Mr Goaway that at the end of the month he will lose his job due to the company having to downsize. Boz feels very uncomfortable as he likes Goaway. He knows Goaway has many financial responsibilities, including a mortgage and family. Losing his job in the current financial climate could be disastrous for Goaway. Boz feels upset but believes he should not show his feelings and be too 'soft', so he covers up with an inappropriate smile. Goaway notices Boz smiling and instead of seeing behind the mask and understanding him as a compassionate and sensitive man, Goaway concludes he is a heartless bastard. This misunderstanding could be a problem for both people. Goaway will feel unappreciated, unsupported by his boss and will not be inspired to deal with this big change in his life. And as Mr Goaway tells others how he was treated, Mr Boz may develop a reputation in the company as being an insensitive and uncaring leader.

AND-DO-IT

Personal Smile Barometer

→ Ask a range of people – a friend, a family member and a colleague – for specific feedback about when you smile.

→ Ask them to let you know if/when your smile is not related to what you are saying.

→ Restrict this feedback to a period of about a week.

If you identify the 'inappropriate smile' as one of your habits, see if you can note when it happens and then replace it with a deep breath and/or a relaxing stretch of your face.

Sometimes just the awareness of its existence can shift the behaviour pattern.

AND-DO-IT
Smile Them

Part One
→ When you walk down the street, deliberately engage in eye contact with a warm smile as you pass people coming the other way. To make sure the smile is genuine, have a positive and curious thought either about that particular person or about anything which makes you feel like smiling.
→ Always keep walking.
→ Vary your choice of age and gender.
→ The response will often be another smile back and depending on the country, ethnic/religious background, and whether you are in the city or the countryside you may even get a hello!

This exercise is not looking at the smile of sexual appreciation and attraction, which has a whole other dynamic and rule system!

Part Two
→ Repeat the above but do not smile...perhaps even grimace.
→ The response from the people you pass by will probably be none or distant.

Both parts could potentially change the level of comfort for you or the other person.
Note if/when that happens.

Under The Skin

1 Habits & Personal Rituals Are Not Who We Are

This section includes two AND-DO-ITs
  ...Wipe that smile...

Luckily a lot of our communication behaviour is habitual. It would be exhausting if we had to constantly re-consider all our physical and vocal possibilities for every action. For example, as we moved from one space to another, if we had to decide whether to walk, crawl, skip, run, or every time we answered the phone we had to decide whether to whisper, speak, shout, sing... then there would be less space for any other thought processes. Our civilising process encourages us to routinely use a repertoire of agreed behaviour patterns. We do this with our personal communication habits and rituals. These are developed from an intricate and unique combination of home, family and friend influences, as well as from our particular culture. The habits and rituals make it easier to survive, fit in and even enjoy...a cup of tea.

CIVILISATION?
A Dry Moment

"Would you like to have a cup of tea?"

*"Yes please
I would like a cup of tea.
Yes
I would like a cup of tea.
With or without you, I would like a cup of tea.
But are you sure,
that you without me,
would really like a cup of tea?"*

*"I don't know
I honestly don't know*

if I, just me,
would like to drink a cup of tea."

"Well then I will let you be.
I will let you wait and see.
If you can find that feeling free
to really want a cup of tea.

And after all I have to say
considering the time of day
and all this talking back and forth
has taken my desire and force
my feeling for a cup of tea
has gone away you see.

So I'll be off
and see you when?
It could be eight or maybe ten.
At least we have not wasted time
in drinking something out of line."

What can happen over the years is that the reason and use for a certain habit becomes out of date and no longer valid. But the habit persists, sometimes turning into a subtle personal prison. For example: at school there might have been a teacher who shouted, *"Wipe that smile off your face Alex, be quiet and sit still!"* And to this day, perhaps thirty years later, Alex might still listen to others with a frozen and unresponsive expression on his face. And this might be (mis)understood as disinterest. It is worth remembering that if we have just met someone, our de-coding may be inaccurate, particularly if they have a lot of out-of-date communication habits. We will not be able to correctly second-guess them and therefore may experience a level of confusion or disbelief. Recently, a client, after listening to me for a while, declared in a flat, bored tone of voice, how interested he was in the EPT ideas. Even with all my experience it was surprisingly hard to believe him. After further questioning it transpired he truly meant it. Many of us are reluctant to change these habits, because we confuse our habitual behaviour with who we think we are. There is that familiar comment: *"I just want to be myself. If I change my behaviour it feels unnatural, it is not me any more!"* These comments may also be backed up with: *"If I have achieved so much with the way I am, why would I even want to change? Why move or talk in a way that feels different and initially uncomfortable?"*

Our physical and vocal development is simultaneous with that of the emotions and the intellect and they become intertwined. For example, if your mother encouraged you to walk in a strong, adventurous way and to fall down and get up with ease, you may be a person who strides into a room with clear confidence and a fast tempo. People around you may like and recognise that as being one of your qualities, part of YOU. But if the same YOU had had a mother who said: *"Be careful, don't fall, watch out,"* you might have learnt to walk in a more careful and seemingly calm way. And your friends and colleagues might appreciate the careful and calm way you came into a room and recognise this as YOU. To change the way you walk may feel as if your personality is at stake. However, being inflexible with habits can also work against you if they are received in a negative light. If you are unaware of this as well as being unable to adjust and change, you may become labelled as a caricature of a particular behaviour pattern: *"Watch out, here comes Miss Speedy."* Or: *"Oh yawn, I have a meeting with Mr Slow!"*

Different ways of behaving: fast or slow, energised or careful and many more are all possible and a useful part of your repertoire of 'YOU'.

In a cross cultural setting to be able to change a behavioural habit or ritual could be vital to the success of an occasion, even in something as basic as the rituals of meeting, greeting and eating together.

Another type of out-of-place or out-of-date behaviour could be more immediate, the residue from your last meeting/experience/encounter with someone else. If, for example, you have just had an irritating conversation with a colleague and then you and I have a meeting, your habit might be to park some of that irritation from the previous meeting in your body, for example with clenched fists or a frown, or in your voice, for example with a tight jaw and brittle resonance. This irritation, which has nothing to do with me, leaks into our relationship and becomes our problem, and our mutual understanding decreases. The UNDERSTANDING GAP increases.

To make sure that emotional tensions do not leak from one meeting to the next in the form of physical and vocal residue, it is useful to refresh yourself in between interactions.

See **AND-DO-IT**: Residue Clean Out, at the end of the section.
In this way we keep our communication clear, accurate and relevant to the people or person we are actually talking with.

AND-DO-IT

The Foot Tapper

Questions to ask a friend, family member or someone you work and regularly talk with:

→ "Please identify for me one physical, vocal habit or repetitive action, which I do, which has nothing to do with the content of what I am saying. For example: your head is always tipped to one side... or your face looks angry when your are concentrating... or your foot is often tapping as if you are irritated... or you often say 'to be honest' just before you note a personal opinion... or you often look away from me when I tell you something important..."

→ Choose one point and ask that person to give you a subtle sign each time they notice you doing it.

→ Replace the out-of-date or disconnected habit with a different action, which could more accurately complement your message at that moment in time.

AND-DO-IT
Residue Clean Out

→ In between one interaction/meeting and the next
→ In between one phone call and the next

1. Take a couple of seconds to shake out your body – perhaps jump in the air – this is a great way to let go for a second.

2. Make a 'throw away' sound, which has nothing to do with talking with anyone.

3. Take an easy, low breath and think about someone you like to be with.

4. Notice something which is actually happening: a smell, a sound, a colour...

2 Identity

This section includes four AND-DO-ITs

...rejecter of 'man's best friend'...

How would you categorise or assess yourself? If I was to say you are a brilliant mathematician, would you agree?

Consider the mathematical calculations involved in walking across a road in the rain. You calculate: the width of the road, the speed of the approaching traffic, if the approaching cars are either increasing or decreasing their speed, the length of your step, the speed of your step, your capacity to increase or decrease the speed and length of your step, the effect of the slipperiness of the shoes you are wearing on the surface of the wet road and how that could affect the speed of your step, the approximate percentage of 'likelihoods' that you fall, the cars skid and so on...

You will not be actually crunching numbers but you will be making a series of complex mathematical calculations assessing speed, distance, and probabilities. Could you re-consider the statement that you are a brilliant mathematician, and if you did not before would you now agree with it?

Being slightly word blind I used to label myself as 'someone who could not spell,' until it was pointed out that about 90% of the words I use, I can spell. So I could change my identity-label to say I am a person who can spell and it would be fine. In other situations this 90% may not be enough for people to accept. We may not consider a pilot who can land the plane 90% of the time, as someone who really knows how to fly. Just as we may not ask someone who can competently cross the road in the rain, to solve a mathematical equation connected to successfully engineering the structure of a bridge.

Animalism

I like cats
(they realise this and head butt me)
I like them even more.
I like cats
their independent nature
those knowing looks
the moments they have lightly bitten and scratched in play.

I like cats

Should I change my identity?
An identity that I have become accustomed to
this liker of cats
this be-friender of feline.
After all I really like cats.

I don't like dogs
(they sense this and taunt me)
I like dogs even less.
I don't like dogs
the smell
the master orientated dependency
the mud, shit
and once when I was 14 a dog bit me.

I don't like dogs

The bite reaction belongs to another time.
The smell, master behaviour, shit remain.
But persistent opinion could provoke another bite.
After all dogs do.
I don't like dogs.

> Should I change this identity?
> This identity which I have become accustomed to.
> This 'Dog disliker'
> this rejecter of 'man's best friend'.
> After all I like cats.

Is your identity defined by what you like? Are you a person who likes cats, a person who likes dogs, or do you like both or neither? It is most probably an easy enough question to reply to. But do you feel attacked or underappreciated when reading the poem if for example you happen to be a dog lover? People have a tendency to identify and feel more comfortable with those who share the same likes and dislikes.

How often do people identify themselves by what they do in the slick title of some kind of profession? If you were, for the fun of it, to choose a profession which is far away from your expertise or interests to define your identity, would others treat you differently? The theme of the mistaken identity is a popular dramatic subject in both films and literature. Last week I spent an evening sitting next to an airline pilot during dinner, and I could not resist picking his brains for the inside stories of his profession. Does our curiosity about someone change depending on what their title and profession is? Is it a way to quickly assess what we may have in common? Does it close the GAP of understanding or does it increase it as we turn that person into a stereotypical representative of a certain job description? Interestingly, some people who have lost their job or retire experience an identity crisis, as their daily existence and interaction with others can no longer be defined by their occupation. Are we what we do? Or do we do what we are?

MEET the MEAT

If a meat hook has never
Actually pierced through
A lump of meat
Can we call it a
Meat Hook?
Maybe
Maybe not.

People also form identities by associating each other and themselves with certain behaviours. For example: *"He is a shy person"* or *"I am a confident person,"* as if they are always that way. People have both shy and confident moments – it is more a question of percentages. What we show and use in any particular situation will be a combination of our behavioural habits and capabilities in juxtaposition with the qualities of the people around us. We also have the capacity to change these behaviour 'identities' and often do. **But** if you decide to behave differently, and it may be something as simple as talking a bit louder to make a point when previously you were always softly spoken, you may find that it really shakes up other people's idea of who you are. And they tell you in no uncertain terms that that way of talking is NOT YOU! As if you are a finished product. In this way, how often do we stop each other from developing, changing, exploring?

Over the years many different methods have been constructed to analyse and categorise an individual's identity. In magazines and on the internet there are innumerable tests anyone can fill in, often in a form of 'yes – no' questions, to find out who they are. Organisations, in a quest to put the right people in the right job, will use a selection of popular and respected systems to categorise, for example, the personality-types of their employees. Although some of these assessments can appear quite interesting and even useful, I have found recipients can feel unfairly trapped by the labels they have been given. Reactions can range from defensive anger, to becoming resigned to the test's results or even using the identity assessment to defend their position. *"I cannot help it, that is just who I am, I am identified as a natural ...."* I have seen when working with groups of people that if they are given the opportunity to explore types of behaviour which they have been told are not part of their repertoire and identity, they end up realising that previously given labels are history. To put it simply: the so-called introvert can learn the skills of being heard and seen, and even find pleasure in it. The so-called extrovert who has been told that their strength lies in their ability to predominantly demonstrate action and opinion can discover the power of silence and stillness.

Try giving people you work and live with the space to break some of their self-imposed or group-imposed identities. Do this yourself so people are not so fast to decide how you will or should behave in any particular role. This can be achieved with quite small behavioural changes. For example: if you are someone who tends to arrive at the last minute for an appointment, vary this. Or if you prefer to arrive well on time to prepare yourself, see what it feels like and how your identity impact changes by arriving just in time! If you are a director and your assistant always serves you coffee, offer to bring them a cup from time to time. If you are a parent and you always keep your eye on the clock when getting everyone ready for school in the morning, give this task to one of the children!

Let yourself have the possibility to expand your identity through altering an action, interaction or responsibility.

The more ease we can develop with changing our behaviour patterns, both within traditional role identities and individual social conditioning, the more we can close GAPs between our day-to-day responsibilities and our creative potential.

Through flexibility and changing behavioural habits we will increase our repertoire of identity. Our acquired tastes, habits or job titles are not who we have to be for the rest of our life.

AND-DO-IT
Expanding the Familiar

Do one thing differently today.
For example:

→ Pick up your cup to drink with the opposite hand than you usually use.

→ Notice that although it may feel strange and unfamiliar it is still you.

→ A 'you' which is evolving.

→ Note some specific details of how it feels different.

AND-DO-IT
Quality Identity

→ Name one quality that people have described you as being.

→ Think of a situation when this was true.

→ Think of another situation when this quality was not evident.

→ Note that in both situations it was you.

AND-DO-IT
Point of Viewing

→ Consider someone you know not only from the point of view of your relationship to them but also from the point of view of someone else's relationship to them.

For example: Your parents are also the son or daughter of their parents.

→ This can help to loosen up our idea of who we think someone is.

Some changes of perspective can be quite challenging For example, I know few people who feel comfortable thinking of their parents being sexual together.

AND-DO-IT
Category Breaker

Break the thinking pattern of your perhaps self-imposed categories.

Behaviour pattern: I sleep with a night light.
Category: I am a person who is afraid of the dark.
or
Category: I am a person who prefers the light.

Exercise a change of category by altering the way you describe a simple action.

This can also change the mental perspective:
Do you *'switch the light on'*, or do you *'turn the darkness off'*?
As my then three-year-old daughter once asked me to do.

3 Authenticity
I/ME & US/WE

This section includes two AND-DO-ITs
   ...or slipping off and hoping I do not miss too much...

A dictionary definition of authenticity is: 'a particular way of dealing with the external world, being faithful to internal rather than external ideas'. However, people often confuse the familiarity and comfort of behavioural habits with a feeling of *'being themselves'* and thus explain that as how to be authentic.

It is recognised that when someone appears authentic, we believe them and if it is their goal, we are more likely to be inspired by their action and thinking. And when someone appears insincere or phoney, we do not believe or trust them. I would like to identify this as the action of BEING = authentic, versus DOING = inauthentic. BEING will have a lot to do with where your 'in the moment' focus is, and if your imagination and emotions are consistently supported by your body and voice. It is the difference between you trying to DO an emotion, for example saying "Thank you for inviting me, it is a pleasure to meet you", whilst really wanting to be watching the football, and actually feeling the emotion which matches your words. These mismatch moments, both on a small and large scale, are common.

In the past few years 'authentic communication' and 'authentic leadership' have become a frequently repeated request and desire from many people I work with. I am curious as to why this is and what people exactly mean by it. The other day a human resources colleague explained that in large companies people increasingly feel overwhelmed by the force and character of the organisation and/or their bosses. There is often a feeling of: *"Where am I in all this?" "Who am I in this context and how can I hang on to my 'real' thoughts and feelings, when I am spending so much time in an environment which is asking me to conform?"* I can imagine how people who are over compliant and supportive to either a boss or an organisation run the risk that everyone thinks their actions and choices are their own. And yet they themselves feel anything but authentic.

Most of our thinking and behaviour is learnt from others, and therefore has many authors. With this unique combination of influences each person makes their choice of elements, to use as their personal knowledge and behaviour base. If we feel that those choices are all too consistently made by others through the must-dos of conformity, then at a certain point we no longer feel like the author of our thoughts and actions. Included in this book are many people's thoughts and ideas but I have made the choice on contents and style, and in this way I feel confident in being able to sign my signature at the end of the document. In daily life can we maintain that signature feeling in the way we live? Or do we feel we are being ghost-written?

Giving up a preferred behaviour can happen for various reasons. A common one is when helping or supporting someone who is ill.

Supporting Jacqueline story

Jacqueline had breast cancer. She was only thirty-six; the cancer was identified as aggressive, fast growing and it had already travelled to the lymph glands in her armpits. The prognosis was not encouraging. She was determined to beat the seeming death sentence and over the next three years went through quite a journey: radiotherapy, chemotherapy, daily meditation, non-carcinogenic and cell healing diets, energy specialists, professional healers, herbalists... A dear friend, Molly, decided to support both Jacqueline and her partner in whichever way they chose to fight the cancer. There were many people around with enough opinions and at the time Molly felt the best thing was simply to consistently support Jacqueline. Molly consciously gave up her own point of view and needs as she felt,
"I can't imagine what it is like to be faced with such a prognosis, so who am I to judge?" Jacqueline was sometimes changing her ideas quite dramatically,

but since she was struggling Molly felt it was more important to help her live with a day-to-day feeling of hope, rather than point out the inconsistencies in her theories. The collateral damage for Molly in giving up her opinion and selflessly supporting Jacqueline was that after Jacqueline died, the partner presumed that Molly's 100% supportive behaviour was still available. The partner had a continued expectation that Molly would agree with every action and idea. To reverse this expectation proved surprisingly complex.

Whatever the demands of a situation or of an individual, it is important to consistently keep in touch with the idea: "What do I want/need/feel? What do I think?" and, if needs be, express this.

In a business setting, it could be as simple as recognising, during a meeting, that I need to go to the toilet. So instead of either holding on and not going to the toilet, or slipping off and hoping I do not miss too much of the meeting, I could say: *"I need to go to the toilet, can we all take a short break?"* or *"Could you put the discussion on hold everyone, until I get back?"* If I ever make this point with a group of professional women, it is amazing how many will nod in recognition, and say they have never dared to ask for something as simple as even this basic need.

It is in everyone's interests that we keep our 'I' in a satisfactory shape. This may seem obvious and yet it is often easy to neglect. When you are sitting on a plane and the air steward(ess) is describing the safety procedure, what do they tell you to do if the oxygen masks drop down? *"First put the oxygen mask on yourself and then if necessary assist the adult or child next to you."* In that context it is clear you cannot help someone else if you yourself have no oxygen. Yet in daily life how often do we neglect to put the metaphorical oxygen mask on ourselves? Ask any parent this question and particularly if she is female the answer will most probably be: *"I constantly forget!"*

The oxygen represents being able to recognise a full spectrum of personal requirements both at home and at work. It means to be able to articulate this to others and if a compromise is necessary, to not pretend otherwise. And lastly, if there are too many compromises for too long, to be able to realise this and as soon as possible do something to change the situation. If you do give yourself oxygen, is it in little bursts each time you notice you need some? A kind of damage repair? Or do you make sure you have a constant and ample supply?

With everything that the oxygen represents, if your supply is constant it means your sense of 'I' is more likely to be in a healthy state. It is useful to cultivate the ambition to nurture your own authenticity in this way. I would describe this as being ambitious. By holding the bar high for yourself in looking after your needs you increase the possibilities to explore your potential. Unfortunately some people (often women) blur the meanings between being personally ambitious and the self-important, ungenerous behaviour displayed by some successful individuals who only think about themselves.

If we starve our 'I' by perhaps too often giving up our perspective and desire consciously, as Molly did with Jacqueline, or subconsciously in the humdrum of daily life, there can be a negative knock-on effect. This can be in the form of self-destructive feelings and behaviour patterns such as lack of motivation, frustration, lethargy, disengagement or even exhaustion. An additional reaction to overextended compliance is that when eventually a person has the possibility to do something their way, an almost stubborn behaviour can set in. Their establishment of 'I' may become rigid, defensive or even covert. You may experience this yourself when suddenly a small choice becomes overly important and out of proportion to the situation. For example, I have to smile as I remember once saying: *"If you borrow my pen, put it back exactly where I left it or don't ever touch it again!"* An over-reaction will come out in not just the content of what someone says but the way they walk, talk and interact.

How can both an individual and a group simultaneously have an authentic existence?

Clearly the character of a group (US/WE) is made up of the combination of individuals (I/ME). Our ease of being able to focus on and balance between the 'I' and the 'WE' can be affected by gender conditioning. It has been noted that with young children, in the northern hemisphere, a girl's first words will often include "We", whereas with boys it will generally be "I". Young girls are encouraged to consider the needs of the group and young boys are often expected to be strong and stand-alone.

This conditioning regularly carries on into the workplace. Recently I was waiting for everyone to return to the conference space after the lunch break to continue the course. One of the participants arrived at the last moment and then proceeded to get some water for herself, and also served her colleagues sitting next to her. I had already put the start of the afternoon session on hold for her, everyone else was ready and waiting. I waited, we waited. As she returned to the table after the initial water serving, since she was being excessively concerned for everyone's well-being, she realised that there were other people in the room who also did not have a bottle of water close at hand. So she then asked if they too would like some water, delaying the start even longer. At this moment, I asked her to really look and see everyone in the room and realise they were all healthy adults and well capable of getting water for themselves.

Her need for kindness, consideration and looking after everyone overrode her ability to notice we were all waiting to start. It was not possible for her to see that her delaying actions were sucking the energy out of the beginning to the afternoon. Over-caring for others, and not clearly seeing and prioritising the 'WE' of a situation, can dramatically reduce a woman's perceived entitlement to a leadership position. Similarly, for men to be considerate and flexible is often perceived by some other men as weak behaviour. It is less usual for a man to look after everyone's need for, say, a glass of water in this kind of way, although more usual as an act of authority and generosity for a man to offer someone a drink. These dynamics are slowly changing as the male and female roles at work and at home are adjusting, but it is a pervasive pattern affecting the 'I' and 'WE' interactions in daily life.

The more individuals are able to look after themselves, whilst still considering the needs of others, the more they will maintain an authentic quality to their behaviour. In turn the group has more of a chance to have a healthy and clear identity. We do not all have to get along and be cosy with each other but we do need to see and be seen, hear and be heard. There is a big difference between: *"I have to do my job, which is to carry out the wishes of my boss or the company with 'pretend discussion' meetings where nobody listens to each other, included in the package."* And a group of people having varying points of view with the space for discussion leading to either a consensus-decision-making structure or the acceptance of a person with the final say. In any group undertaking, if the communication between the group members is at an optimum, if each person feels acknowledged, then with this sense of 'WE' and inclusion it is more likely that the group can effectively focus on the 'IT'. The 'IT' being the subject or reason that the group is working together in the first place.

When social structures give individuals space to develop and express their opinions and choices, it can lead to creative diversity and group authenticity.

Authenticity is created by nourishing both the 'I' and the 'WE'.

AND-DO-IT

Flexible 'I'

→ Notice either at home or at work when you or someone else is being overly **inflexible** about a seemingly small/unimportant issue.

→ Take a moment to think if you or they are having enough regular opportunities to make decisions and exert a sense of 'I'.

→ If this is not the case see what (often small) thing(s) you can change to alter the balance.

AND-DO-IT

Balancing 'I' and 'We'

1. Think of one moment recently when you put your needs before the pressing needs of those around you.

2. Think of one moment recently when you put the needs of others before your own.

   Is there an identifiable difference between the frequency and ease of action 1 and 2?

→ Next time you are required to choose between your needs or point of view and that of others take a moment to make a strategic rather than a habitual decision.

→ If you decide to either stand up for your position or conversely sublimate it, keep a sense of balancing your own needs and those of the group/company/other individual over the longer time line.

→ If you have a leadership position, be it in your family, with friends or at work, notice when someone is over functioning either in 'We' or 'I'. Explore ways to address and change this either with direct questions or with more subtle ways of delegating.

4 Negotiating Self-Worth

This section has two AND-DO-ITs
   ...But is it fair...

When something you do or say is assessed by someone else, is it an accurate indication of value? How about any self-assessment you may make? Is that valuation permanent or transitory? A moment in time. And is the value of what you do the value of who you are? Making this connection can be misleading and confusing.

If we feel as if we only exist when living in the opinion of others, what would happen if everyone stopped thinking about us? It reminds me of that early stage in human development when very young children think as they cover their eyes that no-one can see them any more.

When we do something, make, write or say something, it will probably be perceived by three entities: our self in the moment of action, our 'critical-monkey thoughts' and other people. This inevitably will create a combination of dialogues and opinions around the value of the action. Since one of our survival mechanisms is to be accepted, appreciated and valued by the group, our critical-monkey all too often tries to second-guess the perception of others. This second-guessing will rarely take the shape of self-appreciation or praise. The more familiar form is a replay of negative criticism which we have received in the past. The pull towards listening to those negative monkey thoughts may be rooted in the idea: *"If I can critically analyse my action before anyone else I will outwit or circumvent any negative reactions by others and perhaps be appreciated and valued."*

And if we receive verbal feedback and even appreciation from others, how do we measure it? Does it depend on who it comes from and how often? I have noticed I can feel more valued when receiving praise from someone I respect who rarely gives this to me. It is almost as if a starvation diet of being valued works as an incentive as I get pulled into striving for more. There are enough instances when I have heard a comment like: *"Well if Jan says he likes it then it must be good, he almost never gives a compliment."* Maybe it is like many experiences, if we get too many of them they can lose their potency, if we get too few it can become overly important. Has your sense of value become dependent on any one person's verbal appreciation? How dependent are others on yours? And do you regularly have a personal appreciative chat with yourself?!

Balance critique which is connected to your personal value, with the character and feedback habit of the person who has given it to you.

And what about the next step beyond verbal appreciation? Can an action be measured in a currency of exchange? With friendships we do things for each other within a sophisticated web of transactions. It would probably be received as an insult if you were to offer a friend some money for useful advice or for a delicious dinner at their home. Yet we will create some form of reciprocity, possibly for the dinner by bringing flowers or a bottle of wine, offering to wash up and/or inviting them to eat with us at another time. But in our work most of us will have our actions assessed and then translated into money to be given and received as fair exchange.

Is it fair, can it always be a just repayment?

Most cultures use some kind of currency to pay for services given or for articles acquired. There will often be a specific behaviour to negotiate these transactions. Haggling over an amount is a way of life, a national sport for some countries and an insult in others. Given you know the country you live in and the way transactions are played out, it is helpful to consider your relationship with the thing you have created and the people you are making the exchange with. Remember to differentiate between the value of what you have done or made and your sense of self-worth. The action of exchanging time and expertise for money or even a less immediate payment in the form of a promotion, can sometimes be surprisingly tricky.

Page illustration story
Earning my living as a freelance illustrator/cartoonist meant that each time I made a drawing for a different magazine I had to negotiate the fee. At the time, most magazines would have several standard prices depending on size – full page, half page, quarter page – and whether the drawing was in colour or black and white. Sometimes the magazine would commission a quarter page drawing and then when they went to print it would appear covering a full page. This also happened the other way round. Since this on the whole balanced out, my approach was to be clear about the fee beforehand for the size and detail needed; if their graphic designer then used the drawing otherwise I would leave the fee as originally agreed.

Coming from a middle class English background I often felt slightly uncomfortable talking about money, particularly when it was connected to something I had created. I will never forget the day this changed. I had been commissioned to draw a full page, full colour illustration for the Dutch magazine *Physchologie*, a new client. They had given me the commission a couple of weeks earlier and I was half way through making the illustration. I then realised I could no longer put it off, I had to ring the editor and negotiate the fee before I completed the work. Gingerly I picked up the phone and got him on the line. I announced who I was and said: *"I hate to talk about money, but we need to agree on a fee for the commission you have just given me."* I could feel him smiling at the other end of the line as he declared: *"I have no problem talking about money."* At which moment I realised what a weak and ridiculous position I had just put myself in. I had lost my sense of humour and had become too vulnerable to negotiate. I felt I had to accept his fee proposal, and I did.

"Let us never negotiate out of fear. But let us never fear to negotiate."
John F. Kennedy

My middle class discomfort around money, and the vulnerability which often occurs when I create something, had allowed me to muddle up my feelings of self-worth with the worth of the drawing. The value of me rather than that of the drawing (how much time, effort, talent and skill) was being measured in this case, in money. Ever since, I have found it useful to keep remembering most transactions are not necessarily fairly related to the amount of real time and expertise invested. Sometimes it can feel as if I am underpaid, sometimes overpaid and sometimes it feels just fine! Large amounts of money do not necessarily equal large amounts of worth.

The real value of something often becomes apparent with time. Take something as simple as employing the services of a plumber to mend a leaking tap. Whether their hourly rate is value for money will be linked to the length of time the tap remains drip-free after they have mended it.

To realise what you create is not the sum total of who you are, leads to more confidence and freedom to negotiate.

If we interrupt the flow between a thought or action and the subsequent personal critique it becomes easier to analyse its worth objectively. This holds true as much in discussions as in presenting larger projects.

This process of 'letting it go' is described in the **AND-DO-IT** at the end of the section.

Another issue in the workplace is acknowledging that certain trappings of power will influence the way people receive and appreciate us. Years ago a friend of mine set up his own consultancy business.

He had been used to working for a large company with an equally large salary. Now he had no salary but a lot of experience and wisdom. The question was, besides his impressive CV how could he tempt possible clients into believing his one-man consultancy was of a high quality and that his services were the ones to choose? He decided to invest in a brand new Mercedes. His thinking behind this was that if his potential clients saw the car they would assume he was affluent and successful and therefore good at his job! The strategy worked and he thrived. I have noticed over the years when I had an exhibition of my paintings that the first painting to sell would be the one which was either printed on the invitation or which I reproduced on a postcard. The printing somehow gives people the confidence to buy. Both the expensive car and the postcard give a message of value, a stamp of approval. In some cases an opulent display of success can work against you as it provokes a client to question what you are spending your fees on, and that maybe they are paying you too much! This will depend on the kind of clientele you are targeting. But funnily enough if you quote too low, you can also price yourself out of a job. Sometimes charging a certain amount of money gives others a confidence in you and your services.

In the workplace a perceived value could be in the form of a bigger room or an elevated title on the business card. It can be useful to realise this and even sometimes go along with it. But I believe it is important not to get pulled into thinking that it is who you are and what you are worth.

Woman in the workplace story

Nathalie was puzzling over whether the following situation mattered to her both personally and professionally or not. She had a leadership position and responsibilities in a certain department, which were exactly on a par with a male colleague, Oscar. She noticed that recently Oscar had received his own office and a new job title indicating a rise in position. However, his job and responsibilities remained the same. When she went to her boss and asked about this seeming change of status her boss answered: *"Oh, nothing has really changed. It was important for Oscar to have this so we gave it to him, but his job and yours are of equal importance."* She left the meeting accepting that the change was just an insignificant little tactic to humour Oscar.

The very fact that Nathalie was talking about it indicated to me that it mattered to her. As an experiment I suggested she return to her boss and ask for a similar change in her 'perceived' status in the form of the private office and title change. Without too much negotiation the boss agreed. Nathalie saw that these trappings of advancement changed the way she was treated and respected in the company even though her actual job function had not changed. She was amazed. When we next met I asked her: *"So what about Oscar's salary? Is it the same as yours since you have a similar position?"* It had not occurred to her to even think about this let alone ask. Nathalie loved her job and found it too personal to take a pragmatic look at her market value. However, once we identified that it was not *'the sum total of who she was,'* Nathalie was able to return to her boss and make sure her salary was also in line with others in the company who were holding a similar position of responsibility. To date we can see world-wide that for the same or comparable work, women consistently make less money than men. A sense of self-worth can impact directly on being able to negotiate a higher salary.

Self-worth can also be affected by employment structures which support biased decision-making in the promotion process. The types of people who are under represented in management and executive positions, including qualified females, do not always feel an automatic entitlement to hold positions of leadership. It therefore becomes even more important that they cultivate a feeling of self-worth, independent from the company culture in which they may work, in order to effectively navigate and negotiate both promotion and wage increases.

At times we hold back from publicly valuing what we have done and what we are thinking as we do not want to be seen to be arrogant. But if we sincerely articulate the worth of what we are thinking and doing with physical and vocal expression in line with the content, then it is more likely that it will be received in the same spirit. This in turn may not only encourage others to appreciate their own qualities in an honest, open and public way, but also inspire them to use and develop their talents.

Notice the difference between arrogance and dignity by identifying the distinction between showing off at the expense of others and – in a generous way – tooting your own horn.

AND-DO-IT
Money & Worth

Think of three situations when you have received money for work and:

1. You felt you received a correct payment.

2. You felt underpaid.

3. You felt overpaid.

→ Put the three actions side by side and evaluate.

→ Is there any difference in the quality of your input?

→ Is there any difference in your feeling of self-worth?

AND-DO-IT
Let It Go

In the workplace try using the following sequence:

1. Immediately after you have completed a certain action or spoken thought, resist analysing and count to 5 in your head.

2. Then see if you can notice the value reaction in others.

3. Then consider your own value perception.

4. Does it match up?

5. Does it matter?

6. Smile to yourself. And remember that this is an action or idea – it is not the total sum of who you are.

5 Meeting as Equals

This section includes two AND-DO-ITs

...and slightly creepy...

Pedestal story

It was my first year at Dartington College of Arts, studying the performing arts. Me eighteen, a city kid from London, straight from school, ready and hungry to explore and experiment.

Dartington was renowned for its alternative and experimental approach to the arts. The college, located in the middle of a beautiful country estate in the south of England, was isolated from the rest of the world. It was, to say the least, a rarefied atmosphere. We had a group of inspiring tutors and one in particular had just arrived from New York. He had even studied and worked in Poland with the legendary theatre maker Jerzy Grotowski. DAVIDd, male, mid-thirties, was impressive, and we were impressionable. All the other tutors had a much more 1970s laid-back, Tao-influenced approach to teaching. But the New Yorker DAVIDd, athletic, short black hair, short black beard, black Buddy Holly style glasses, straight talking with rarely a smile, was the person who shook us all up. During those first months at college he was the tutor who most of the students talked about.

Just before the end of the first term and the Christmas break, we each had a short report and tutorial from our teachers. I sat there opposite this hero listening to his analysis of me. In a New Yorker's drawl he explained: *"You know Jessie... I have never had a student quite so disturbed as you... I think you should go and do some therapy during this coming holiday... why not try Gestalt therapy... my wife does that... it seems to be effective..."* This was a complete surprise. It seemed to come out of nowhere. To prove his point he used an example of something I had done during an improvisation class, and by taking it out of context made my action indeed appear extreme and strange. Because I admired him I did not immediately see the GAPs in his logic. To this day I can still puzzle about why he tried to demolish me. Was it because I was quite cheeky and from time to time would make a joke in an attempt to get him to lighten up, crack his cool exterior? This teacher, who I respected and believed, had more or less told me I was mad; so I walked out of the meeting thinking that maybe I was! I went home a couple of days later. During the Christmas holidays I immediately started reading Frits Perls' books about Gestalt therapy. And, as advised, I joined a Gestalt therapy group, travelling up to the centre of London each day to reclaim the sanity which my teacher had convinced me I had lost. It was an interesting process and during that week I gradually realised it was not me who was disturbed, not at all. I had a pretty balanced view on life for an eighteen-year-old. But the person who was not only irresponsible but also rather unstable was DAVIDd.

I returned to college liberated from the negative influence of this careless teacher. It was strange as most of my friends continued to place this man on a pedestal. But as the next two years progressed, it became clearer to others that although on many levels DAVIDd was talented and inspiring, he was also nuts. In spite of himself DAVIDd taught me a valuable life lesson. Since that time, regardless of anyone's apparent social position and expertise, whether they are the CEO of a multinational or a young child in a playground, I meet them with a similar mixture of curiosity, respect and perspective.

A feeling of meeting as equals. Their opinion is just that... 'their opinion'.

About ten years later I was in New York. One evening after attending a performance at the La MaMa Theater I bumped into DAVIDd in the foyer. He looked similar, an older version of the same style. To my surprise, he was delighted to see me and insisted on joining me and my friends for a drink. After he finally left, my friends asked: *"Who on earth was that strange, nervous and slightly creepy man?"* This meeting and their comments were a confirmation of what I had realised all those years earlier as a student.

In all situations involving meeting with one or more people, we listen and talk with different qualities of confidence. This will probably

depend on how we position ourselves relative to them, connected to a real or imagined power structure. Money and possessions, a decision-making position, knowledge, age, gender, sexuality, religion, family, culture, nationality, ethnic background...

We experience changing 'personal-position' dynamics from the earliest moments of our lives: the vulnerability and dependency of a baby, the rivalry of siblings, the power of a teacher, the dominance of an institution, peer group pressure... These and many other types of personal positioning continue on into our adult situations during work, at home and at leisure. The individual subterranean mechanisms, which keep these dances in place, are intricate. So assuming they will constantly try to play a part in your relationships, it is valuable to regularly note how you are positioning yourself with other people.

If you use proactive curiosity, you are more likely to bypass an often inaccurate, projected idea of who you think someone might be. And experience them with clarity as potentially interesting and unrelated to your personal sense of self-worth.

A more open, interesting and flexible communication atmosphere is created. The GAP closes. As well as changing your own outlook, this can also free up the other person's sense of themselves. This curiosity can be extended even into situations and people who you would rather not encounter. Sometimes remarkably interesting and inspiring ideas come as a result of a seemingly unpleasant situation. Or through interaction with a person you do not like or are even in conflict with, as in the case of DAVIDd.

Sustaining curiosity helps to close the GAP if not with the other people at least with an ease with yourself.

Whatever our so-called status may be in this world, we are all human beings who are born, live and finally die.

AND-DO-IT

Look Up - Look Down

Choose one example of each of the following groups, and find a photograph if you have one.

- → One of your parents.
- → A teacher you did not like from your childhood.
- → A 'best' friend from your childhood.
- → A colleague you enjoy working with.
- → A shopkeeper or waiter who has recently served you.
- → A film star you are attracted to.
- → A head of state you admire.
- → A politician you distrust.
- → A child you love.

Once you have chosen an example from each category then, one by one, imagine you are with each of them meeting them personally and offering them something to drink.

With the first three, see them from the point of view of yourself as a child. And the rest from an adult's point of view.

After each thought note if are you looking up to them, down to them or feel on an equal level.

Repeat the imagination exercise and focus on remaining curious towards them as a human being without any need to either elevate or diminish their status in relationship to yourself.

Note any differences in yourself.

AND-DO-IT
Levelling the Playing Field

Each time you meet with someone you believe is 'superior' to yourself, or has more perceived power than you:

→ Firstly notice if this is restricting you in some way.

→ Notice if you feel some form of nervousness and therefore cannot think so clearly or behave so freely.

→ Then remember they too need to eat, sleep, go to the toilet...

Use the same principle with someone you do not like or who you feel has less status or perceived power than yourself.

6 Conscious of Self Versus Self-Conscious

This section includes two AND-DO-ITs

...strange collection of misfits could actually play...

Rock band story

In the late 1970s the performer side of me had a chance to live out another dream: play the bass guitar in a rock band. Together with my friend Colen, who had an amazing singing voice, and his friend Tsuneo Matsumoto, a Japanese lead guitarist with hair to his waist, who played like Jimi Hendrix, we formed the band FLEX. An almost constantly stoned drummer, whose name I no longer remember, completed the foursome. Through some connections we lined up a tour to be the support band on the comeback tour of the Atomic Rooster (a well known band in the UK, from the early 1970s). Our first gig was in the Midlands of England. It was early winter, the drive long and rainy, and the location unwelcoming. When we arrived we discovered that two support bands had been booked by mistake. As we all sat huddled together in the small changing room – walls covered in aggressive swear words and sexually explicit graffiti, stinking of years of spilt beer and vomit – the other support band, well seasoned and arrogant, looked at us with distaste. Colen, slightly built and androgynous; Tsuneo, Japanese; and me, lower than low, a female bass guitarist (at that time females in bands were mostly only singers). Which group was going to be the warm-up band that evening, them or us? Eventually we agreed to both play, and guess who got the weakest and first spot of the evening? We were the first to go on stage. The hall was huge, dark and cold, the air humming with the smell of alcohol and cigarette smoke. The audience were mainly already drunk bikers in leather jackets who were bored and impatient. So you can imagine as we walked out on stage to plug in and tune up (there had been no sound check) the reception from the hall was somewhat cold and predatory.

Up until then the only time I had been on stage in front of a large audience was as an actor. This meant that I was portraying someone other than myself. I had not realised until that moment what an enormous difference there was between acting and being on stage just as myself. (Some musicians deal with this by creating a performing persona, for example David Bowie and Ziggy Stardust.) The other problem was that I could only play if I was completely sober, so I could not seek the comfort and Dutch courage of alcohol. I felt so vulnerable, adrenaline and fear were mounting by the second. If I did not do something about it, I knew I would end up shaking so much that even the simplest of chords would slip through my fingers.

Probably out of pure terror there were two things I instinctively did which saved me, and indeed have supported me in moments of fear ever since.

Firstly: 'As If' behaviour.
I thought: what do bass guitarists do and look like when they first appear on stage?
→ They take the guitar – so I slung it over my body and plugged it into the amplifier.
→ They look cool and laid back – I imagined that I had drunk a few beers.
→ They check the tuning and feel of the instrument – I adjusted the volume, tuned up and played a few riffs.

By doing this, I claimed the stage and established a relationship with my colleagues and the guitar. I had re-found some kind of identity and started to breathe again. But then I looked into the darkness and fear gripped me again as I considered: are they thinking about me...what are they thinking about me...what will they think of the band? We are going to be massacred!

It was then I experienced the second change of perspective: 'Outward Questioning'.
→ I moved my attention around and thought: what do I think of the audience?
→ I wondered who they were...where did they come from...how did they mostly enjoy an evening's entertainment..?

So by (1) establishing my Bass Guitarist identity with a few physical actions and (2) coupling this with thinking about the audience rather than about myself, I immediately calmed down and gained the mental space to perform. I could move forward.

Those two ways of thinking freed me to be perceptive, receptive and creative. We played with guts and originality. The audience could not believe their ears and at the end of our set they did not want us to leave the stage. Much to the surprise and resentment of the other two bands, we, the strange collection of misfits, could actually play!

After that initial tour, peaking with our last gig at the Marquee in London, a notorious venue where many bands including the Rolling Stones, Jimi Hendrix, The Who, Led Zeppelin, Genesis and the Moody Blues had played, FLEX disbanded. We all had other priorities. I had lived out a dream to play the bass guitar in a rock band. To carry on and make a full-time lifestyle out of it was, for me, not necessary.

Over the following years I have kept noticing that if I begin to feel overly self conscious, and worry about what people are thinking of me, I become disconnected from what is actually happening. The fear also creates a GAP between myself and my ability to interact. If I do not do anything about it, this GAP with my own potential steadily increases. My private critical voice starts to pump more and more self-deprecating ideas about what I guess others may be thinking about me. If this ever starts to happen it is important to 'nip it in the bud'. Steer self-critical thoughts towards, firstly, non-judgemental physical observations about oneself, for example: *'My feet are on the ground, I am breathing.'* And secondly turn curiosity out towards the other people, remembering to keep to quite simple thoughts like: *'I wonder what he ate for breakfast?'* or *'What kind of music does she enjoy?'* Thus considering the humanness of these people in a wider context. This turns my attention away from myself and enables me to engage with them as fellow-humans.

By coupling these two ways of thinking you become conscious of yourself and more conscious of the situation in a non-judgemental, curious and creative way. This will also create a feeling of self-confidence.

AND-DO-IT
Tasting 'As If'

'As If' behaviour: Each time you walk into a room in the next few days try out thinking one of the following thoughts:

1. I am six years old and have just eaten a big cream cake.

2. I am cold and tired.

3. I have just won a million dollars.

4. I have lost my way.

5. I am surrounded by people who appreciate me.

6. No-one will ever understand what I am trying to do here.

7. I am on holiday.

Notice how you feel with the different thoughts and if there is a difference in how people react/interact with you.

AND-DO-IT

Flexing the Curiosity Muscle

Perceive with an open mind without trying to decide what other people may be thinking about you. You will anyway most probably get it wrong!

→ Next time you have to articulate your ideas and opinions to a group of people who will not necessarily agree or even appreciate you, if at any time you start to worry about being rejected:

1. Have a small thought about your physical reality, for example: what temperature are my hands?

2. Move your focus to the group and have playful and specific curious thoughts about some of them.

7 Fearless or Fearful

This section has two AND-DO-ITs

...trying to prove your case...

If you were to wake up and think, *"Today I am going to experience fear,"* would you think *"Great!"* or *"Oh dear rather not"*?

If we never experienced fear we would probably not live past the first few years of our life. For example if I burn myself on the stove, then the next time I am near the stove and one of the flames is ignited I will probably be more careful than I was before the burn. In this way we build up knowledge around a variety of dangerous and less dangerous experiences. This helps us to make increasingly complex assessments of any given situation.

So fear is a friend. Unfortunately it can also become a tricky alliance as some of our encounters with fear end up becoming triggers to minor or even major traumas. Returning to the burn example. It could be that I become very badly burnt, ending up in hospital, and after this whenever I come near fire it creates an unstoppable panic feeling inside me. It could then mean throughout my life, whenever I have to do anything connected with fire, I feel frightened and therefore try to avoid the situation.

Or perhaps once when I was a child as I stood too close to the stove my mother became furious with me, and for several years forbade me to go near a stove at all. In which case the stove may feel unnecessarily dangerous to me. Consequently as an adult I may be so fearful that I dare not even go near a stove, and therefore become unable to cook! Conversely, in an attempt to overcome my fear and prove I am no longer scared, I may come too close to the heat and burn myself. As the fear has become so out of proportion I am unable to realistically assess the danger of the situation. The trouble with this type of fear is that even if we try to press on through and use the stove we may be so nervous that indeed some kind of accident does happen. This then reinforces the fearfulness and a repetitive cycle establishes itself.

Sometimes we decide not to see dangerous situations or refuse to take them into account as we want to appear fearless to others. It could be something simple like overtaking a car when we cannot really see enough into the distance to make a safe calculation. Do we for a second not care if we injure or kill anyone including ourselves? Are we showing off, or have we watched so much violence on television that we have become detached from the shocking reality of accidents and pain?

Backbone story

I was once in a theatre piece where we presented ourselves as the 'Linton Family Wrestlers'. The set was a wrestling ring, the characters were a mother, father, son and daughter. I played the mother. The performance was made up of fighting scenes from different family dynamics spliced with actual wrestling. We did a lot of research and worked with a professional wrestler who taught us a repertoire of different holds and throws. There was a moment in the show where I was thrown through the air over one of my colleagues. It was a throw which frightened me. But being tough and twenty-four years old I refused to admit it was a problem. On one occasion we were performing in an outdoor summer theatre festival in Bath, a city in the UK. We had warmed up our bodies and were ready for the show, which was booked for eight o'clock Unfortunately we had to wait until about nine before starting, by which time it had become darker and colder and the muscles in our bodies were no longer ready and tuned for the athletic movements.

We did the show and during that particular throw I felt myself once more slightly fear it. As my fellow actor threw me through the air my muscles tensed with the unresolved fear and my body hit the floor of the wrestling ring with a slight twist and an extra heavy thump. The show went on, the show must always go on! That evening we partied and went to bed. The next day I could not get out of bed without someone helping me sit up first. I managed to get to a doctor, who directed me immediately to hospital. I had broken the transverse processes on one of my lower vertebrae and cracked a few ribs. I had to lie on my back for six weeks until the bones healed.

This was a major lesson concerning listening to fear. It did not make me physically fearful but it did help me to keep looking at what my personal motivation is for taking risks and when an unresolved fear could stop me from assessing clearly.

Do we all have to break our backs to learn that some fears need to be listened to? Hopefully not. But what we do need to do is balance our ambition with our ability. And realise when and how to find out more knowledge to support our desires.

Our fears can also be connected to emotional accidents.

Moving to an example in the workplace. Imagine that last week you had a meeting with Mr Stormoff and he, without pulling any punches, rejected your report. You have meanwhile licked your wounds and today have a new meeting with him. You have rewritten the report and sharpened up the proposal in an attempt to move forward. If you go into this meeting fearing that he will once again humiliate you and reject your proposal, you will be less likely to notice if he changes his opinion and explains how he loves the report and congratulates you on your ingenuity. If you are in fearful-mode you will probably either not hear him or not believe him and consequently carry on trying to prove your case. At a certain point Mr Stormoff may wonder why you are not pleased to hear he is giving the budget you asked for. As you oversell the idea he may even begin to mistrust you. The meeting could end up with him retracting his offer and suggesting you go away and re-work the proposal one more time. In this way your fear of rejection has been realised.

Fear can keep us out of time present perception, batting us back and forth between *"Oh I hope that does not happen again"*, *"I wish that other thing would happen"*, *"I am not prepared enough, I am not good enough... I am not enough..."*

What fear can give us is useful information. It is just a question of recognising the difference between valuable signs right now, associations with personal historical pain which could cloud our evaluation, and a fear of rejection or failure.

We can be warriors going into challenging situations with curiosity, ready to do anything, trusting that we can handle it one way or another. Or we can be worriers, fearing a repetition of hurtful past experiences, thinking: *"I will not be able to succeed."*

If fearfulness determines your responses then you may wonder how many of those plentiful choices you are really considering.

AND-DO-IT
Shifting Fearful

Use the information fear gives you as just that, information, and return to focussing on the situation.

Direct your thoughts to cover the following:

→ Curiosity – resist forming conclusions or judgements.

→ Trust your experience.

→ Let go of the past and future 'worry' thoughts.

→ Focus your senses (sight, hearing, smell, taste, touch) in time present.

→ Interact with what is actually happening.

This will shift your initial fear reaction. The UNDERSTANDING GAP between the real situation and your fearful perception reduces.

AND-DO-IT
Turning the Worry-Mode off

On a daily basis, notice when you are worrying, or feeling fearful about anything at all. Give it a 1 to 10 order of importance, smile to yourself and take one of the following actions:

1. If the fear is valid, take note and act accordingly.
2. If you really need to continue analysing the 'worry', attempt to put it in perspective.
3. Use the following exercises to move your thoughts and awareness onto something else.

Some simple and fast ways to turn the *'what if'* worry-mode off:

Ask yourself some real questions about time present.
For example:
→ Am I breathing constantly or holding my breath?
→ What smells can I smell?
→ If my feet are on the ground, what are the varying pressures under my feet?
→ Can I feel a smile on my face, in my stomach?

Then
→ Make a tight fist with both hands and let them go loose and floppy.
→ If there are other people in the room, note a specific detail about them, for example the shape of their eyebrows.

8 When Taking Risks Is Motivating & Inspiring

This section contains two AND-DO-ITs

...voyeuristic and too uncomfortable to proceed...

Have you ever seen a trapeze act at the circus or on television? When does it become exciting, boring, or maybe impossible to watch? As they swing and let go to be caught by their partner, why is it exhilarating if they take a risk? It could be that they almost miss each other's hands or they perform such a complicated twist and somersault in freefall that as they reach for the rope they catch it by a hair's breadth. If they performed these movements and easily caught each other or the rope, would we enjoy the performance as much as when we could see them taking a risk, almost falling? Many people prefer to see them take the risk. If however the trapeze artist fell to their death would we enjoy that too? Probably not. Two elements which enable us to enjoy seeing them take the risk are, firstly, seeing that they have technique and experience, and secondly, knowing they have a safety cord attached to their harness, or there is a safety net underneath them. We can then enjoy them pushing the limits. The combination of skills and knowledge plus the safety net or cord are deciding factors. If we see someone taking a risk without these elements, we may feel uncomfortable. We may even not want to be in the same space as that person. We feel a big desire for a BIG GAP between us.

Sometimes we may perceive a risk when we see an individual doing something which is, for them, emotionally uncomfortable. Interestingly, their feeling of insecurity and discomfort may have nothing to do with their actual talents and abilities.

Naked man story

As a group of art students were setting up their easels and getting ready to work for the morning life class, an extraordinarily beautiful young man stepped onto the small rostrum, slipped off his gown and sat in a pose suggested by the teacher. He was shy, and clearly felt very uncomfortable sitting in the room completely naked. And this in front of about twenty people who were looking closely at him in an attempt to accurately draw his naked body. One of the students, Clare, started to draw but each time she looked at him, she felt that the personal risk he was taking was more than he could handle. Although he had an inspiring body and she would love to have drawn it, she could not look at him as he was so self conscious. It felt voyeuristic and too uncomfortable to proceed. She ended up drawing something else in the room. After the class was over Clare discussed her reaction with some of the other students. To her surprise and also relief she found that they had all had similar reactions, though they had dealt with it in different ways.

Since the young man could not bear to be looked at and had no personal resources to help him become at ease with the situation, the students in turn could not bear to look at him. The personal risk which he was taking was uninspiring. Sometimes just admitting that a situation is personally risky, and perhaps asking for support, can be enough. For example, if the young man in the life class had been able to say that he felt uncomfortable and self conscious it might have lifted the atmosphere. This could have made it easier for everyone to draw him whilst at the same time appreciating the personal risk he was taking.

People holding leadership positions often tell me that they feel it is far too risky and definitely a sign of weakness to say *"I don't know."* A simple emotional safety net in such a case is to realise that in spite of everyone's expectations, it is sometimes necessary, and can even be inspiring, to have the confidence to say: *"I don't know...what do you think?"* It takes a mature person to do this when their job title and responsibilities are suggesting they should know the 'right' answer to everything in a certain area of expertise. Whenever I have experienced someone daring to take this risk, it has proved inspiring to the rest of the group.

Risk-taking in the realm of communication and leadership can be inspiring for ourselves as well as others when we develop various skills and knowledge safety nets combined with some kind of emotional safety net. The emotional safety net could be a close group of friends with whom you can confide and create mutual support, someone agreeing to be your ally during a particular meeting, a personal coach, sponsor, mentor. Or it could be a sequence of thoughts, for example the AND-DO-IT: Turn the Worry-Mode off, described in the section: Fearless or Fearful?

In this way we can take the emotional and intellectual risks that bring people to another level of interaction and discovery without it becoming personally destructive or just plain embarrassing.

A practical safety net for leadership and communication moments when the pressure is on, is to give yourself a moment of sensitivity to reflect on why and how to proceed. There are several short techniques described in this book which can give you this. For example in Golden Classics section on Silence, the **AND-DO-IT**: Elastic Silence.

AND-DO-IT

Sensitivity to Reflect on Risk

When something feels physically, emotionally or intellectually dangerous, create an in-the-moment space in your mind to be able to assess taking a risk:

→ **Check if you have enough Knowledge, Technique and Experience to challenge your capabilities.**
If you feel any doubt, assess what could be a realistic consequence of the action.
What have you or others got to lose?

→ **Identify feelings**
Identify any strong feelings and whether they are reasonable and logical.

Get to know the difference between the adrenaline rush of anticipation and strong feelings of doubt and fear. Remember that to proceed with an action when you are experiencing a storm of feelings, whether reasonable or not, will cloud your judgement and affect your abilities.

Then decide to do one or more of the following:
1. **Accept the possible loss and take an intelligent risk.**
2. **Become more informed/skilled.**
3. **Describe your doubts and ask for help.**

AND-DO-IT
Taking a Stance

1. In unimportant interactions/situations when either an opinion or a decision is asked of you, experiment with the following:

   Dare to clearly choose and say YES or NO or I DON'T KNOW

   This action in itself can sometimes feel like a risk. It can also be inspiring if, **without apology**, we simply dare to declare our position.

2. Once you have gained confidence with how this works, extend the idea to more important situations.

9 Pleasure

This section contains one AND-DO-IT

...Kissing is kissing...

How do we find and re-find that feeling when time seems to stand still, the GAP closes and we feel in the centre of our existence? There is a difference between that and the other time-standing-still feeling, when for example you are driving somewhere and your destination from being a hundred kilometres away is suddenly just around the corner. That I would describe as lost time. This can be experienced as a relief if you are tired and wanting to get to your destination, or it can create an uncomfortable feeling of being in a time warp: *"Where did the last hour go to?"* These days a common situation where this can happen is on the internet.

But the other sensation of losing the inner chatter and purely experiencing, feels glorious. I have tasted this during different activities: reading a book, listening to music, dancing to music, sex, sport, rare moments during meditating, and coaching executives. Then there are the so-called creative activities: playing music, drawing, painting, writing, acting. The feeling is definitely connected to being extremely focussed on time present. Ironically, when we focus on time present in this way, we sometimes lose a clear notion of time.

For me it came down to one of the creative processes where I know I can consistently re-find that very alive feeling. After I studied theatre and then spent many years as a theatre maker, I moved to the solitary profession of visual art. One of the personal motivators for making this change was that I then had the independence to choose to create or not. I no longer had to be reliant on all the factors which have to be in place before a theatre performance can happen: the script, director, designer, fellow-actors, location, technicians, audience and...money.

So yes, painting did it for me. The only thing that could stop me was myself, and over the past thirty-five years I have consistently returned to the action of putting shapes on paper or canvas. I find that if there is too much time between one session in my studio and another I become short tempered, irritated. For years I felt that this unique feeling which I managed to journey towards and kept re-finding when I was in my studio painting, was connected to the ambiguous quest of closing the personal GAP of self meeting self, through creativity. And I felt I needed it on a regular basis.

Then a couple of years ago I was reading an article in the *New Scientist* magazine about the state of human happiness. It described how every day the left and right hemispheres of the brain interact with each other through electrical and chemical nerve impulses. To put it simply, the right cerebral hemisphere responds to and decodes feelings and more intuitive perceptions, and the left side tends to be more analytical. Often a person will be either more right or left hemisphere dominated in their general thinking and behaviour patterns. The article said that the more there is a balance of both types of thinking, resulting in a regular exchange between both hemispheres of the brain, the happier we feel. It then went on to describe specific activities which tend to create this state of being, which included certain types of sport and music (Bach is a favourite). Music has a mathematical structure and yet also contains emotional interpretation. Therefore the left and right hemispheres are interacting intensively as we listen. I realised that this is exactly what happens to me when I am painting. I will take an analytical, philosophical and stylistic idea. Then I let that float as I respond to my feelings of pleasure to do with form, shape and the colour of the paint. The two ways of thinking then continuously interact and trade off dominance. So my ethereal and sometimes mystical feelings about *'needing to paint'* are in fact linked to a chemical and electrical exchange between two sections of my brain, which create a pleasure factor.

Once realised, we can apply this understanding more knowingly to any activity. I believe this is particularly relevant in business, where the analytical side of our brain is given so much acknowledgement and priority. It is important to proactively bring in the balance. If you think about the people you want to work with it is probably the individuals who are not only skilled and informed but who also have a certain amount of ease, awareness, and pleasure in their job. Those who have an ability to combine sharp thinking with a spectrum of interactive emotions are a pleasure to be with.

In business it has become popular to have 'team building' or 'bonding' events where a group of people are taken out of the business context into a more informal environment to experience a playful or sporty activity together. It is recognised that when individuals show more sides of their personalities in this way, the pleasure and creative thinking of the group increases. The same principle applies when groups of people go away to a retreat for a few days to 'brainstorm' together.

If each person can keep the pleasure principle going throughout the day by balancing their analytical and emotional thinking patterns, then the need for one of those damage repair events to re-ignite or re-inspire the office, although often fun, becomes less pressing. The same idea can extend towards creating new business relations and collaborations. If you are a pleasure to be with, people are more likely to want to collaborate with you.

If you are not enjoying yourself that much on a daily basis, why not? What are you waiting for? The end of the day? The weekend? The yearly holiday? This is your life now, every minute of every day. If you don't decide to do something about it and just wait for the moments of pleasure which are given to you on a random basis in life, you may have a long wait coming.

And Painting

Park bench
A couple
Tumbling tongues
Kissing

Centuries of variations on the theme:
two mouths
two tongues
and so on.

Kissing
is
Kissing
The structure the same.
The difference the delight.

TONGUE (tung), n. Muscular organ in the mouth used in tasting, masticating and swallowing, and speaking, faculty or manner of speaking, (arch.) a language.

KISS, n. Caress given with lips; (billiards) impact between two balls.

(Pocket Oxford)

And Painting

AND-DO-IT
Finding the Feel-Good Factor

Take any action, for example eating an apple pie.
As you are eating, alter the way you experience the action by changing your perspective:

→ Smell the aroma, feel the texture, taste the taste as you are chewing and swallowing it.

→ Analyse its contents: what kind of apples, how much flour, butter and so on?

→ Have an opinion about its quality. Is it as tasty as the last apple pie you ate?

→ Talk with friends about something other than apple pies. Or if you are alone let your mind wander to other thoughts.

If you make sure that you regularly change the focus of your perception you can come closer to that wonderful 'alert in the middle of your being' experience, and therefore establish a higher feel-good factor! It will also be more likely that people will want to collaborate with you.

10 Balance As a Verb

This section includes one referred AND-DO-IT
    ...gripping...gripping – less...sliding accelerating...

There is a lot of talk these days about how important it is to achieve a work-life balance. In today's economy dual-income couples are usually the norm, in order to make ends meet. Should a couple decide to have children it often presents an organisational pressure that feels impossible to handle comfortably. They are faced with how to cover the care for their children 24/7 as well as working an 8+/- hour day.

Without going into a sociological analysis of the breakdown of our extended families, and with it the organic community support systems, I would like to look at what happens if both parents have a full time job. Or, as is also increasingly the norm, there is a single parent. If you are lucky enough to have a grandparent living close by who is willing and able to help out with child-care, all well and good. However, many parents are faced with the practical and emotional dilemma of how to provide quality care for their children, and at the same time maintain their career and income. The practical options open to most are: professional child-care facilities such as a crèche, amateur child minders (often older school kids or retired women), family, friends and neighbours on an ad hoc basis, live-in nannies and au pairs, other parents.

There are several problems with this list. One is the organisational difficulty of matching the availability and capacity of the child-care services with the parents' jobs. Another is that usually these services cost money, sometimes so much money that once subtracted it almost cancels out the extra earned by one of the working parents. And then there is the emotional feeling of guilt, particularly for professional women. The expectation for so many years has been that a 'good' mother looks after the children herself. The woman will often feel that she is not a good-enough mother; and also not a good-enough professional since she does not have limitless time to work extra hours or work-socialise. Similarly, some men may feel that to be a 'good' father they should be earning the money for the entire family, and so they are letting the side down. The consequence being: both parents may feel they are not good-enough parents or good-enough professionals.

As the social pressure for women to be readily available for their children at all times can be so great, if they are working full-time there is often a strong pull to compensate for their absence. We can call this 'super-woman syndrome'. They feel that if they cannot be there themselves then at least they will organise it well, and consequently take the lion's share of running the household. Some women may do this with ease but generally it is mission impossible, and as well as exhaustion, resentment can build up between the parents. Each feels as if the other is either not doing enough or doing too much and therefore making the other feel guilty.

These days for anyone who is personally ambitious, whether they are a parent or not, there are a multitude of actions and desires to choose between. Many people feel bombarded with the responsibilities and never ending 'must-do's of life. With the explosion of communication media in the form of mobile phones and the internet it is easy to get sucked into the need to respond and engage 24/7. It is remarkable how hard it is for executives to turn their phones off during meetings, and in breaks the rush to check emails is obsessive. People are made to feel they are not a good-enough professional if they are not constantly hooked into this way of interacting, and so they never stop working. The seemingly friendly gift from the company of the laptop or latest smart phone has created a modern day tyranny.

Then some specialist comes along and says that everyone needs to find a healthy balance between their work and private life. Many people then approach this goal of finding a work-life balance as just that:

an end result, to be achieved or not. And apparently, to remain healthy, once the balance is achieved you must not lose it. As to maintain continuous balance is impossible, and as we either do not realise this or do not admit it, a feeling of perpetual failure and guilt can run rampant.

If you were to stand up and stand still for a moment, you could describe that as successfully achieving physical balance. If I was to ask you to keep that state of balance as just balance, what cannot happen? You would not be able to walk. The very action of walking requires that you push yourself into imbalance and then with ease re-find balance. By repeating this sequence you walk.

Unfortunately balance usually has the 'good press' and imbalance the 'bad press'. But we cannot have one without the other. Balance is part of a process. Think of balance as an action, as a verb.

Many actions happen through the combination of balance and imbalance. If either of these states lasts for too long or too short a time the process of the action will probably break down. Sometimes there are natural limits that will catch us, for example if I stay out of balance too long in the walking action I will probably fall to the ground. This fall may have no more consequences than a bruised ego or a twisted ankle. Sometimes the consequences may be more destructive, for example when walking along a mountain path with a sheer drop on one side of you. If we take this as a metaphor for our daily life, it is helpful to consider from situation to situation when it is best to take smaller or larger risks with the extremes of balancing.

We can take the walking example and relate it to many of our daily experiences, whether we have children or not. If we realise that balance is a passing moment between imbalances it makes it so much easier to enjoy the constant change and required re-adjustments of daily life. Balancing.

It will also help us to be kinder to ourselves when we realise that losing a moment of balance is inevitable and even desirable if we wish to develop. The UNDERSTANDING GAP reduces (and with me the sense of humour increases) if we give up trying to achieve the impossible. In the workplace a tool that can help those of us who have a demanding job, is to regularly take a bird's eye view of those insistent requests and responsibilities. Take moments to pause, prioritise and adjust. Notice what this gives you, develop the desire and feel the right to have these moments to listen to your needs as well as those of the company. So you, your colleagues, friends and family can enjoy and participate in the balancing.

Bird Balancing

Balancing on a slanting glass roof
The bird chooses to walk a metal support
To take the incline

Gripping
Gripping – less
Sliding
Accelerating
Claws clutching

And then with a breath the bird spreads its wings and flies from view
Scraping claws echoing lift-off
Balancing into the air.

In Golden Classics section, Flexibility with Holding On & Letting Go, see the AND-DO-IT: Walk the Talk.

11 Wholes and Holes

This section includes one AND-DO-IT

...absence of a double you...

How often do you feel you have the freedom to choose to show any side of yourself rather than the situation making the choice for you? Consider the different qualities and parts of yourself which you display: at work, talking with your parents, socialising with friends and family, on holiday, having breakfast in your pyjamas, at the gym or jogging in the park.

In each different setting you will probably experience slightly different versions of yourself. We often adapt ourselves to fit into each situation without even thinking about it. The adaptation could be simply the clothes we choose to wear, for example wearing smart business clothes rather than pyjamas when attending an important meeting. It could be the way we choose to talk, walk and so on. Our choices are hopefully wise, but consider the difference between the two following approaches to the same choice.

Approach One: **MUST BE**
→ I have to wear these smart clothes rather than my pyjamas, otherwise I will not be accepted, fit in or be taken seriously.

→ I have to keep quiet rather than express my opinion in this meeting, as everyone is more senior than me.

Approach Two: **CHOOSE TO BE**
→ Strategically it is probably the most effective if I wear these smart clothes, but if I wanted to, I could wear my pyjamas and feel fine.

→ Strategically in this particular meeting I choose not to say anything, but if I wanted to, I could.

Approach One is probably how most of us adapt to social situation pressure. This is when we feel there is a part of ourselves which will not be accepted and therefore must not be shown. It can take up a lot of personal energy. If we spend a great deal of our time in the mode of 'I must not', 'I should not', 'I'd better not'...it becomes exhausting. In many companies, and particularly in large organisations, the corporate culture, departmental culture or boss culture can make people feel they must hide all the parts of themselves which seem not to fit in. This constant self-editing creates an uninspiring personal prison.

Approach Two, which may very often result in the same choice of action, gives a sense of personal freedom, energy and even fun.

By repeating the approach described in the **AND-DO-IT**: Choose To Be, you can start to build a whole YOU in any situation rather than feeling obliged to cut yourself up into many parts with holes in between the part of YOU which is allowed in one situation and the part of YOU which is allowed in another!

A whole..A hole

The absence of a double you (W) turns the word into an opposite.
Something complete versus absence.
A space created by absence.

And when you get a lot of holes, you or it are full of holiness,
A Godly state implying wholeness.

Filling the gaps
Creating the holes
Holes invite filling, movement, exchange.
Constant attention to keep on connecting
Keep on connecting, connecting the wholes.

Holes, on the whole, not a great reputation:
'A hole you fall into'
'A hole in your theory'
'A hole in the ozone'
'A hole in your shirt'

Some holes become voids
Panic – suck in – fill quickly
Whirlwind breakage
Call in the Red Cross.

But choosing holes as connectors
Points in their own right
Relating our wholes
Makes a whole without holes.

AND-DO-IT

Choose to Be

During the next week each time you change your social environment, for example going from your home to your workplace, notice if you are in 'Must be' or 'Choose to be' mode.

Choose to be: This is me strategically deciding to censor a part of myself.
or
Must be: There will be a serious problem if I do not comply.

→   If you can identify a bit of 'Must be', smile to yourself and change to 'Choose to be.'

→   Note the difference between a stubborn "I am going to be 'me', if people do not like it that is their problem" approach, and the more playful.... "Mmmmm let's see which sides of me I choose to show!"

By changing your approach to 'Choose to be' you may find that you include more variations of your personal expression.

No Man's Land

1 Past . Present . Future

This section contains two AND-DO-ITs

...Watson, you idiot...

Which state do you choose to spend most of your time in: WAS, IS or WANNABE? And do you even choose?

WAS

There WAS once
And that is the most extraordinary thing there was.
WAS, was often a worrier.
Thinking about and sometimes fearing
instead of enjoying the warmth of the fire.
FLAMES BURN THOUGHT WAS.

WAS spent many pointless hours
trying to reshape the already has happened.
Was it always like this?

You see WAS
there go the burning flames again!

WAS didn't exactly get burnt
but didn't get warm either.
Just too far away
tiptoeing, shivering on the edge of the time-line.

Not seeing that it was
the centre-line in the middle of the road.

That was when the truck came.

The question is was WAS was?

IS

IS is pure is.
IS always is.

Funny really.
When we try to look back
IS isn't there.

IS knows this.
And however deep and delicious
the bites are,
IS leaves no trace.

WANNABE

WANNABE wants to be.
But no-one sees WANNABE
because WANNABE isn't.

WANNABE flaps around
in the storms and waterfalls of dreams.
Hopping from a hoping,
to a I want
to a what if
to a may be.

The ever greener grass on the other side keeps
WANNABE perpetually moving.
Moving towards the if onlys of desire.
And WANNABE will never know if any of this ever happens,
because WANNABE isn't.

Our consciousness is mostly driven by a combination of *remembering* our past experience (from which we may build our strategy/choices), *experiencing* our present time and *imagining* our future plans and desires. The analytical brain will most probably have received a lot of encouragement and, when successful, praise. It will all too often take a dominant role in our awareness, tending to focus the majority of our thinking on past memories and future aspirations: *'what I have had'* and *'what I have done'*, *'what I want to have'* and *'what I want to do.'* The *'what is actually happening'* will often be pushed to the side. How often have you been in a meeting or social gathering and felt that some of the people were like empty bodies just sitting there, their minds absorbed in the past or the future? How often do you experience this yourself, drifting off into the land of memories, analysis and plans?

To learn from past experience is vital. Desires and plans for the future can be reasons and motivations for action, but our only tangible reality is time present. Now is NOW. It is in present time where we find our strongest and most inspiring connection with one another, and this kind of connection can lead to brilliant and innovatory ideas. But we seem to find it hard to live this way. This is probably why so many religions and philosophies have emphasised its importance.

Disconnection story

In the 1970s, when I was acting with the Pip Simmons Theatre Company, one of the shows we developed and performed for about a year was called 'Towards a Nuclear Future'. This was a rather gloomy sociopolitical piece expanding on the idea of what would happen to the fabric of society after a nuclear holocaust. It also examined, given the number of nuclear power plants and the way they were being run and maintained, the likelihood of this happening. We did a lot of research around the subject and in the show included details about questionable behaviour and policies, for example the story of Karen Silkwood (some years later Hollywood made a film featuring this story). Each evening I went through the re-enactment of anger, desolation and sadness. I was completely immersed in the ideas and since we performed almost every day for several months this began to have a lasting effect on me, carrying on after the show finished each night. This steadily built up until I was beginning to feel quite numb and empty throughout the day. I was aware of the change as if a shadow was hanging over me. My friends and director began to be concerned. But it seemed as if there was a chasm between me and the rest of the world, and there was nothing I could do about it. Each day I was struggling in this strange state of disconnection and each evening reinforcing it with yet another show. The numbness was gradually deepening. I knew I had to do something to pull myself out from the past observations and future predictions of this theatre piece, which were becoming my permanent emotional reality. But I was stuck.

I do not remember if I was walking down a road passing some flowers by the wayside, or sitting at a table which had a vase of flowers on it, but somehow my attention was caught by the detail of a single bloom. I started to follow the extraordinary intricacy of its structure with my eyes. The design and beauty of it absorbed and amazed me. As I continued to look at its contours the cage of numbness, which I had become locked into, began to dissolve. A feeling that life, although complex, was extraordinary and enjoyable returned to me. I have used this as a tool ever since, focussing my attention on the reality of something in time present, particularly if I have a lot of pressure around me.

Regular focus on time present is a way to increase awareness. It is also necessary if we wish to be able to pick up relevant information in any meeting we have with other people. And it is vital if we want to reduce the UNDERSTANDING GAPs between us. But perhaps more importantly it is also a key to our sanity. In a complex life where we are handling so many things on so many levels it is the tiny, often fleeting moments of smelling the seasons in the air, the coffee brewing, the bread baking, hearing the wind in the trees, the sound of someone's voice, seeing the wag of a tail, light and shadow on the wall... which will bring us back to a moment of simplicity and straightforward pleasure. In this process the GAP between our consciousness and what we see and feel within ourselves also reduces. The more we can put our constant past and future thoughts on the pause button and re-engage in simple details of now, the more we will give ourselves a bit of mental peace. It focusses our mind. We will then have more mental space to be receptive to valuable information. The information which is often right in front of our nose, and if noticed enables us to make the best moment-to-moment decisions and choices.

To exercise and balance your knowledge, experience, hope and desires with your ever-changing time present perceptions, you need to be able to guide and choose which layer of information to focus on at any given moment. This is just a matter of deciding to exercise changing focus, over and over again until it becomes a familiar thought pattern.

To miss what is actually happening in the moment can mean that all your wealth of experience, knowledge and ambitions will be of little consequence. The following joke puts this idea in a nutshell:

> Sherlock Holmes and Dr Watson were going camping.
>
> They pitched their tent under the stars and went to sleep.
>
> Sometime in the middle of the night Holmes woke Watson up and said:
>
> *"Watson, look up at the stars, and tell me what you see."*
>
> Watson replied: *"I see millions and millions of stars."*
>
> Holmes said: *"And what do you deduce from that?"*

Watson replied: "Well, if there are millions of stars, and if even a few of those have planets, it's quite likely there are some planets like Earth out there. And if there are a few planets like Earth out there, there might also be life."

And Holmes said: *"Watson, you idiot, it means that somebody stole our tent."*

AND-DO-IT

Perception Bouncing - Things

→ Look at something in your room right now, for example this book. Take a few minutes to notice as many details about it as you can see: texture, colour, weight, smell, fingertip feel. **Stay looking, resist analysing.**

→ Now remember the same details of another book you have read in the past weeks, and notice the difference regarding experiencing detail and information.

→ Now imagine a book that you would like to read in the future. Once again how much detailed information can you access?

This exercise can be done with anything. If you are outside look at a tree, car, building...

You will probably find that you receive the greatest amount of vivid information when you are actually looking at your chosen object. Perhaps an obvious conclusion, but keep realising how little of your attention on a daily basis is focussed on the now.

To become familiar with deciding what and how you perceive, regularly play with this exercise any time, any place.

AND-DO-IT

Perception Bouncing - Situations

Have a specific thought about:

1. Details of a moment from the past.

2. Details of something which is happening to you right now: smell, sounds, light...

3. Details of a future desire. It can be quite simple... I want to have lunch in 5 minutes.

   Keep going through the 3 different types of thoughts for a few rounds.

   Becoming limber with these different forms of thinking and perceiving will help you navigate complex discussions with more ease.

2 Intuition & Gut (re-) Action

This section contains one AND-DO-IT

...checking it for a break-in...

When making a decision, have you ever found your intuitive gut feeling immediately leading you to choosing decision **ZZ**? Then your analytical side stops you from taking action by whispering something like: *"Hey wait a minute, to make a good decision we need to look at more reports and a few flow charts."* You listen to these invading questions and after making a thorough analysis of the information you decide to choose solution **XX**. Then a few weeks later it becomes clear that **ZZ** would have been a better choice. But you did not listen to your intuition. It seems hard to make decisions based on a gut or intuitive feeling. This may be because we do not immediately have any substantial information to back up the feeling. Most people have had an education which is information driven. So something like intuition seems mysterious and not to be trusted.

Intuition: The act or faculty of knowing or sensing without the use of rational processes; immediate cognition.
Intuition: Instinctive and unconscious knowing without deduction or reasoning.

In most situations we absorb huge amounts of information at the speed of light. When we have a gut feeling it will probably be based on a multitude of observations which are too subtle and fast for us to analyse in a rational way. In any interaction everyone will make micro movements, sounds and smells, which will stimulate a subconscious response in us. One reason why it is hard to listen to these gut feelings may be because the information is unreliable. The feeling is sometimes spot on and sometimes way off! For example, you may not feel comfortable with someone because they have a certain tone in their voice that is similar to a person who earlier in your life let you down. Or you may feel uneasy because subconsciously you see, hear and smell a collection of signs, which accurately suggest to you this person is nervous and may be hiding essential information from you. So when to trust and act on your intuition and when to rely on your analytical process?

I believe it is useful to have a partnership between our analytical and intuitive perception. Neither perception is greater or lesser than the other, they can both be very useful if given the appropriate status. But the balance of that partnership needs to be continually tested. If I walk into a meeting I may have a strong intuitive sense as to which people have read the report, and I may not have to actually ask everyone. This can create an exciting atmosphere of sensitivity from me towards the group. I can always then test my gut feeling by a few well-placed questions. It is often easier to listen to these intuitive feelings when we give ourselves a bit of space around them.

To lose confidence or belief in our intuition can crush our ability to thrive. It can become quite a handicap.

> **Phone call story**
> Petra and Sam were building a life together. From time to time when the telephone rang at home and Petra answered it, the person at the other end would put the receiver down. She felt a bit spooked by this, and would wonder if someone was watching the house and checking for the possibility of a break-in. When she talked with Sam about it he dismissed the calls as probably a wrong number. This happened in phases, for months it would not occur and then it would start up again. From time to time Petra also considered the possibility that this was another woman. And she even sometimes casually threw that into the pot of possibilities. Sam's responses would be variations of denial, often with a slant towards throwing the focus back on to her: *"You are being paranoid."* It later turned out that he had indeed been having an affair, and the phone calls were from that woman. What damaged Petra the most was that deep down she had known all along. Maybe because she had so wanted the relationship to succeed, Petra let Sam in subtle ways

undermine her trust in her own intuition. She realised that he had not only de-sensitised her perception within their relationship but this had also seeped into her confidence in being able to assess situations in other areas of her life. A feeling of insecurity with any intuitive perceptions continued for quite a time after this relationship finished.

Intuition is a survival mechanism. It is not only to do with our interaction with other people but it also helps us feel the danger or safety of the physical world. Is this building sound, this boat strong, this car safe, this storm dangerous? It works within our negotiations: how much of this information can I trust and which bits, if possible, should I check on? When I take my car to my garage there is a limit to how much I can check to see if they have actually done what I get billed for. My trust in the work builds up from a combination of perceptions: the fact that the car runs well after they have given it a service, my intuitive feeling towards the mechanics as individuals, together with the way I feel that the garage is being run as a whole enterprise.

We can take the car/garage example into any situation where we have to decide on a certain action, be it choosing which school to send our child to, which product to buy, person to employ, job to apply for, or company to invest in. It will be our intuition which, even when we are presented with convincing and so called foolproof data, will 'smell a rat'. If we listen to it, it will make a healthy counterbalance to the oh so dominating and over congratulated cognitive part of our brain.

Situations where it can get hard to follow an intuitive perception are often during collaborations when we wish to persuade others to make a certain choice. In an analytical discussion it will probably not hold much weight if you back up your opinion with the comment: *"I just have a gut feeling that this is the best decision."* If you are surrounded by a group of particularly left cerebral hemisphere orientated thinkers it could even discredit your authority on a certain issue.

One of my graphic designer friends, who is director of a design company which specialises in packaging, commented on how big the UNDERSTANDING GAP can become when presenting his company's new design to a client. If the client asks: *"Why did you use that colour red with that typeface on the crisp pack?"* they will usually not respond well to the reply: *"We have a gut feeling that this is the most impactful design."* They will be much happier with a response like: *"Considering the xxxx research and the xxxx data our specific choice of this red and that typeface will stimulate xxxx percentage of the population to buy your crisps."*

With creative processes – whether it is creating a visual design, writing a piece of music, experimenting with chemicals in a laboratory or exploring an innovatory concept – many ideas and decisions are arrived at through intuition. Depending on our experience and knowledge it is usually safe to trust it, but we may have to backtrack and find a few facts and figures if we need or wish to convince others of our choice. However, I have found if I present an intuitive choice with enough authority and conviction, using clear communication skills, I can inspire others to also take that leap of faith and join me. After all, even seemingly provable facts may not turn out to be as sound and reliable as we would like to believe.

To make a rounded, continually perceptive analysis leading to first-rate decisions, we need to remain alert, responding to intuitive as well as analytical input.

AND-DO-IT
Intuition Tester

Test how you make certain decisions and when/how you use your intuition.

Choose one action/decision to look at more closely:
For example, when buying apples, how do you choose them?

Do you make a choice purely out of habit, without considering anything or anyone, always going for the same variety of apple?

Next time you buy fruit, for example apples take time to:
→ Look and see which apples appear to be the best today, which ones spontaneously appeal to you.

→ Touch them and feel their consistency.

→ Notice what other people are buying.

→ Ask the shopkeeper's advice.

→ Then make a swift decision based on a combination of the above intuitive and rational perceptions.

Try this same structure with various types of action-decisions, including the daily decisions of when to say what...

3 Non-Judgemental Perception & Positive Re-Enforcement Lead to Creativity

This section includes three AND-DO-ITs
...Our brain registers the DOPAMINE JACKPOT...

How often have you received corrective comments related to what is an acceptable way to behave and succeed? How often have these comments been negative?

When these comments from the past replay in the form of a negative loop-tape inside our head, they can block us being able to make intelligent and creative decisions. In versatile ways those judgements which have been thrown at us throughout our life take hold: *"Don't do it like that"*... *"It is all your fault"*... *"If you carry on like this you will fail..."*

Inner negative comments can be crippling; they create a private jail. And if you become trapped in that jail, you may well find yourself dishing out the same kind of crushing criticism to others. It is a pervasive leadership style.

If we use the techniques described in Under The Skin section: Conscious of Self Versus Self-Conscious, to silence or ignore the negative inner comments and give ourselves the freedom to explore what is really happening, it can be amazing what other things we start to notice.

When you are in a meeting and the response is not according to your plan, or in your view even negative, it is easy enough to think: *"I am a failure, and everyone must think I am an idiot."* If you get caught in that black hole, you will probably experience a loss of confidence or ability to think clearly. You may even start to create the very situation you feared. Try instead saying to yourself: *"Mmmmmmm this does not seem to be going very well, I wonder why, let's try another approach..."* Stay in a state of **curiosity** and **flexibility**, keeping in mind that there are many other ways to achieve a similar objective. Then you are more likely to respond sensitively, noticing interesting and important details. When I realise I have been tempted into a negative spiral, I smile to myself and think: *"Jessie! In the history of the universe how important is this?"* The thought instantly puts most situations in proportion for me.

When I am painting a canvas, the moment I analyse the painting in the form of a judgement connected to either success or failure I am lost, and the sharp in-the-moment creative process closes down. When we can keep returning to the thought that **life is a process not an occasion**, with each moment and situation adding to the learning curve, it can optimise the creativity with which we approach problem solving. With the responsibility of leadership will come an additional pressure to succeed, which if we let it gives even less space for curiosity, flexibility and creativity.

We can support creative action and thinking by getting into the habit of giving proactive positive feedback to ourselves as well as each other. In both cases it is important to **identify and be specific** in the appreciation.

If you say to someone: *"That was good, I liked the way you described your ideas during the meeting,"* this gives no tangible information to help them understand why you liked what they said. By saying 'good', you are putting a one-dimensional value label on it connected to your personal taste. They will probably be pleased that you liked it, but being specific is more useful in promoting creative development. For example: *"You were so clear in that last meeting, using moments of silence gave me the time and space to really follow and consider your proposal. Thank you."*

The **positive** element of feedback is easy enough to give either to ourselves or others when we feel positive, but how can we motivate others to collaborate more effectively when we are finding it hard to understand or even be in the same room as them? For example, if a colleague is regularly checking emails during meetings, creating a restless fragmented atmosphere, but sometimes they are focussed and clearly part of the meeting, you could say:

"Please stop checking your emails the whole time, it is driving me crazy!"
Or you could say:
"It gives the discussion more focus when you are able to fully take part, I find your input valuable."

If we feel unappreciated and impelled to put the brakes on an action or change a behaviour pattern through fear of reprimand, the resulting change will be less effective, and unlikely to last in any meaningful way. People will be more inspired to consider change if they first feel recognised for their effort and ability in the form of positive reinforcement. Similarly, if you have gone into a personal negative spiral, taking a moment to specifically identify something about yourself which is positive can help you 'get out of jail free'.

When we experience something which gives us any kind of pleasure, our body produces a chemical called dopamine. Some of that dopamine travels to the area of the brain where memories are formed and creates a memory connecting that action with getting a reward of 'pleasure'. Our brain registers the DOPAMINE JACKPOT. On top of creating memories, dopamine controls the area of the brain responsible for desire, decision-making and motivation. So once an action has hit the dopamine jackpot, the next time your receive a stimulus for this action, your brain receives a surge of dopamine which increases your drive to do it. When you succeed your brain produces even more dopamine, which reinforces the memory and embeds it further in your brain. The more you do something that is or has been rewarding the more dopamine makes sure you do it again. This is precisely how habits and indeed addictions form. This is why it is hard to change a habit even when it is unproductive or self-destructive once it has established this pleasure circuit. Doing so means fighting a fundamental neurological system in the brain.

So how can we change an unproductive habitual behaviour which we have become addicted to? If we give ourselves conscious appreciation for behaviour change, then the dopamine system can engage and our brain will associate pleasure with the new action. Repeating the action with positive reinforcement will lead us to embed fresh, more beneficial behaviour patterns.

How and when can we give motivating feedback which is also critical? How to couple appreciation with points to change?

We often fall into the trap of mixing the two comments together in one sentence or breath. You may say, all in one tone:

*"What a skilfully researched report! You have obviously spent a lot of time on it **BUT** I think the second section needs revising before we can go to print."*

Consider timing. If you talk straight through without a pause and without changing the emotion between the two types of comments, the person will probably not hear the genuine compliment (see Golden Classics section: Giving and Receiving). They are more likely to focus on the *'it is not perfect'* point, and feel unappreciated or demotivated. To change your emotional tone, and leave a couple of seconds, or even wait until another meeting between a positive comment and the critical *'this needs to change'* comment, is more likely to motivate and inspire a person to proceed. For example, you could enthusiastically say:

"What a skilfully researched report! You have obviously spent a lot of time on it, thank you."

See the person receive the compliment and perhaps talk briefly about specific strong points in the report.

Pause, and then change your emotion to, for example, empathy.

"Before we go to print I have some questions which I would like to discuss with you concerning the second section. It may need a bit more work on it."

Giving space and attention to a compliment means that the person is more likely to actually hear it and really feel their effort has been recognised and appreciated. It gives them that feel-good dopamine moment! Then they are more likely to be open to carry on or re-do something, which a few moments earlier they may have believed they had completed. They will be pulled towards seeking more dopamine moments in the form of additional appreciation.

If we can free ourselves from the negative critical voice that tells us we must achieve a right, perfect or finished state, and make our overriding impulse a state of exploration, just experimenting freely as well as knowledgeably, then we can tap into the natural creativity and intelligent, sharp perception that we are all born with.

This is not to say that learning well-tried techniques from other people is a waste of time. However, it is worth remembering that rules are only useful for as long as they are relevant. To keep re-thinking, re-visiting and challenging them is how we evolve.

Perfection?

If you finish...it
Perfectly complete...it
Then any possibility after that point is denied
If you over complete your perception
Are you not
For that moment
Robbing others of potential
By the perfection of your completion
Is it not a massacre of future possibilities?

- is the unfinished state life itself?
or
- is a complete moment without future peace itself?

Has not the full stop...got
a lot to answer for?

AND-DO-IT
Kill the Monkey

→ Notice when there is a 'critical monkey' sitting on your shoulder which starts whispering negative perceptions.

→ Take a moment to pause.

→ Smile.

→ Immediately counterbalance it with a positive perception about yourself.

AND-DO-IT
Appreciation Appreciation

→ Make sure that you regularly give your family, friends and colleagues positive feedback/appreciation.

→ Base each comment on real qualities that you see in them. Make it precise and genuine.

→ Notice the ongoing effect this may have on them.

AND-DO-IT
Positive Plus Change

When you want to both give appreciation and suggest change, experiment with the following approach:

1. Give the compliment. Make sure the person really hears you and receives the compliment. This means that the person needs to say in words or a gesture: *"Thanks."* If they say something like: *"Oh yes, I am glad you liked it but..."* or... *"Yes I spent a lot of time on it but..."* or they start considering what they think about your compliment rather than just receiving it, then they have not metaphorically caught the compliment-ball.

2. Help them to first receive the comment as just your opinion. They do not have to agree or disagree, just receive. Their own analysis, agreement or disagreement can follow later.

3. Repeat if necessary, focussing your thoughts only on that point...make sure that you have no unspoken 'buts' hanging in the air.

4. Have a moment of silence, and see if they are digesting the comment.

5. Alter your emotional tone and state the possible changes which you want to discuss.

4 Right or Wrong... Good or Bad

This section has one AND-DO-IT
    ... likely to experience varying percentages ...

Most of us are taught from an early age that things are right or wrong, correct or incorrect, good or bad. The daily news regularly refers to the good and bad, right and wrong decisions of our leaders. Sometimes today's *'good leadership decision'* morphs into tomorrow's *'lack of vision and irresponsibly wrong actions'*.

Schooling systems worldwide are constructed around passing exams. Particularly for young people up to the age of eighteen, these exams will be made up of questions which have answers that are either correct or incorrect. The correct answer gets the points and we pass the exam, too many wrong answers and we fail. For years many of us will have been finely tuned towards trying to get the 'right' answer. If we get enough 'right' answers we are led to believe more opportunities in life will be available for us. These exams are a simplistic way to find out how much each of us has retained from our lessons. They decide if we know and understand enough to proceed to the next level. If we do not fill in enough 'right' answers to progress through the system, we sometimes get an opportunity to try again and sometimes we do not.

Once we are getting our full time education from life, the categories become less evident as we see there are many effective ways to assess a situation or solve a problem. Unfortunately those years in the schooling system will leave a strong pull to the *'must get it right'* mentality. I continually come across this way of thinking when working with executives since a lot of their success originated from getting top marks at school and university.

This conditioning that there is only one chance and that there is a 'right' answer which you must get if you want to succeed, makes great friends with the fearful feeling. Regularly when I asked my young daughter how she had got on in a test at school, if she had not got 100% right, she would reply in a dejected tone: *"Oh I got two questions wrong"* (out of thirty). The test results were always assessed on the number of incorrect answers given by the student. This negative feedback built up in her as she started to worry more and more about the possibility of getting anything wrong. I tried to help her maintain her confidence, discussing ideas such as: *"How many correct answers did you give?" "What have you learnt from this?"* or *"How could you do it differently next time?"* There is a huge amount of pressure to be 'perfect', and some people end up feeling that if they fall short of that, their very identity is 'bad'. I got it wrong...I am wrong. Once labelled it can be surprisingly hard to shift negative memories and opinions.

This building up of fear and insecurity is connected to what the neuropsychologist Rick Hanson calls *'the brain's negativity bias'*. As we experience something negative our nervous system is hard-wired to instantly remember similar so called failures or near disasters. We have various types of memories. The procedural memory is the one that remembers where you put your keys, the time of an appointment or when and how to shake hands when meeting someone. We also have an emotional memory which is responsible for assigning a feeling tone to stimuli in the brain. This tells us to approach or avoid. It is located in the ancient, reptilian and early mammalian parts of the brain and is primed to instantly label, react to and store experiences as threatening or dangerous. It is a tool which evolved to anticipate and overcome dangers, protect us from pain, and solve problems, so dangers, pain and problems are what capture its attention. For thousands of years this has been a useful part of our survival mechanism.

This negative-emotion reaction registers, compares and responds to negative events almost instantaneously, whereas it takes five to twenty seconds even to begin to register and categorise positive experiences. You may have noticed this pattern: as you consider one personal failure, many related ones from your past can rush back into your consciousness.

Negative and fearful thoughts not only seem to breed but can dominate our memory, as we fixate on the one negative moment of a past meeting or occasion.

In my early twenties, I was fascinated by philosophical ideas about truth and reality. It is interesting to examine why we get drawn into labelling certain perceptions as being right or wrong, correct or incorrect.

Imagine there are just the two of us in a room. We are sitting at a table and between us is a cup. One side of the cup is blue and the other side is white. My reality is a blue cup. Your reality is a white cup. As far as we are concerned we are both seeing the same cup. If we were both asked to describe the cup our descriptions of the same cup would be different yet as far as each of us was concerned we would both be telling the truth. Giving the right answer. My truth of the cup maintains my perspective and your truth of the cup maintains your perspective. There is also an innate truth of the cup. The truth of the cup is the cup.

We can add another layer. I see my perspective of the cup, then stand up and move over to the other side of the table. Now, seeing the cup from your side, my description of the cup will expand, probably taking into consideration your point of view. Your description could either stay the same or be influenced by my changed perception. You might choose to stay where you are and only consider your point of view, or my movement and new description could inspire you to take the view of the other side of the cup into consideration. You might simply trust what I have said about it, or get up and move round to my side of the table to see for yourself. In this way both our realities will have changed.

But the truth of the cup remains the cup, no-one can fully perceive the truth of cup-ness.

In business we are constantly juggling a lot of information and then, usually under pressure, needing to make a 'good' or 'right' decision. And yet we know the information and opinions that we have to take into account are rarely clean-cut, black and white. We are more likely to experience varying percentages of rightness or wrongness.

It strikes me in discussions, whether it is with friends or family, or during business meetings, that there will regularly be someone (including myself sometimes) who declares an 'absolute' point of view. Really believing that in that particular instance what they say is 'right'. Once this standpoint has been declared it can be hard for the individual to step down, admit that there are other possibilities. It can even feel frightening to do so, as if one's very identity is at stake.

GIANTS

A child walks
A landscape of legs
To see
To grow
To walk
Amongst legs
Looking up to where the voices come from.
Legs as thick as small tree trunks
A forest in a room moving
As the child moves through
Towards a desire.

And we say to children: *"Giants don't really exist"*
Whilst
Giants only exist, when we are very young.

All we can attempt to do is describe as clearly as we can our point of view, with the flexibility to keep open to, and even accept, someone else's interpretation of the so called same thing. Then, if necessary, live with the differences, continue to ask questions and realise no-one will be able to fully know. With this approach sticking to the labels of right, wrong, good or bad becomes less relevant.

This brings to mind the word **curiosity**. Accepting different points of view can lead us to be curious about other aspects of life, rather than making assumptions based on those labels. Some of mankind's greatest discoveries have occurred when someone made a 'mistake' and then either they or someone else, instead of trying to right the wrong, was curious enough to investigate what had happened. A famous example of this is Alexander Fleming's discovery of penicillin. He apparently recalled: *"When I woke up just after dawn on 3rd September 1928, I certainly didn't plan to revolutionise all medicine by discovering the world's first antibiotic, or bacteria killer...but I guess that was exactly what I did."*

In September 1928, Fleming returned to his laboratory having spent August on holiday with his family. Before leaving he had stacked all his cultures of staphylococci on a bench in a corner of his laboratory. On returning, Fleming noticed that one culture was contaminated with a fungus. If he had had a strong pull to do everything in the 'right' way he might have thought: *'This is wrong, as a good scientist I should have tidied up after my experiment. I will clean these dishes as they are no longer useful to the experiment I had in mind.'* Luckily he had a more curious approach to this 'accident': he allowed himself to run with the unexpected. And therefore noticed that the colonies of staphylococci which immediately surrounded the fungus had been destroyed, whereas other colonies further away were normal. Later Fleming identified the mould which had contaminated his culture plates as being from the *Penicillium* genus, and – after some months of calling it 'mould juice' – named the substance it released as Penicillin on 7th March 1929.

Our hard-wired 'brain negativity bias' coupled with the influence of the 'right or wrong' approach in our education can act as a shield, preventing us seeing what is actually happening. When under either self inflicted or external pressures, the brain is not necessarily an organ for objectively studying reality. Unbiased curiosity will need active encouragement.

AND-DO-IT
Right/Wrong Pause Button

During the next few days note:

1. Three times when you strongly want people to agree with your point of view or course of action.

2. Three times when you let go of what you believe to be 'right' and observe from another person's point of view.

3. Three times when you resist the pull to form or express an opinion and maintain curiosity.

   Note the feelings connected to these occasions.

   Try balancing these different points of view when you formulate leadership decisions.

5 Trust & Belief

This section contains three AND-DO-ITs
...in the flash of a moment...

There is an aphorism: trust is earned. In our crowded, complex society, we have even made some trust-earning a legal requirement. For example, we earn the trust of others if we drive, by passing a driving test. Have you ever driven in a country where the requirement to pass a driving test is easy-going or non-existent? In my experience the feeling of trust towards my fellow drivers is dramatically reduced. And yet the amount of trust we display with or without the test, as we hurtle down a motorway, is still massive. I have noticed that immediately a fellow car or lorry driver makes the slightest unconventional move, for example veering slightly out of their lane for no apparent reason, my trust reduces and I become more alert.

I am grateful that society has built up a series of structures so that I can trust that the buildings I live in and go into have been designed and built by architects, engineers and builders who have proved that they know what they are doing. We sometimes hear tragic stories where this is not the case, for example in earthquake areas where professionals, by taking cheap shortcuts and not following the legal requirements of design and construction, have not only broken the law but also society's trust in them. Then, when the earthquake strikes, a school collapses, killing hundreds of children.

Another profession in which we put a considerable amount of trust is the medical profession. If you have ever had to visit a hospital or doctors' practice, can you remember the varying levels of trust that you have felt towards different individuals? That feeling will probably not only come from the content of your conversation. It will also develop from the way they talk with you, the timbre of their voice, the ease of their body and the direction and length of their gaze. The confusing thing is that being a skilled communicator does not automatically make them an expert and dextrous surgeon. Similarly just because someone has passed a test it does not mean they are truly an expert in that field. What is the pull in blindly trusting a figure of authority? Is it because they are just that, with either the correct diplomas hanging on the wall or a convincing demeanour or both? Is it because we feel vulnerable, desperately wanting them, in the case of the doctor, to sort out our health and make everything OK?

We are all born helpless, with no option but to trust the adults around us. And yet these people often behave in illogical and contradictory ways. So as we grow older it can become confusing to decode their actions and possibly hard to continue extending unconditional trust and belief. For example, a three-year-old runs into the road after a ball, and his father screams at him to stop as he sees a car speeding in his son's direction. After the incident the child might not understand why his father continues to shout and be angry with him. He will probably not realise his father's anger is an expression of fear and love. If the father does not quite rapidly explain his screaming and anger and give his son a big warm, loving hug and a kiss, the child may start to fear his father and trust him a little less. Similar small *'trust accidents'* will commonly happen throughout each person's childhood.

When someone betrays a trust which we have put in them, it may be hard to rebuild it. If it only happens once, and is something small like denying eating the last biscuit on the plate, we can shrug it off. But if someone consistently breaks our trust, it builds up until it becomes impossible to do anything together since it will be hard to believe what they say. In personal relationships the people close to us are probably the ones we trust the most. If this fundamental trust is broken it can feel as if our whole emotional world is collapsing.

Fear and lack of trust can sometimes occur when we cannot understand or decode someone's behaviour, simply because they are not like ourselves. They may be different in the way they look, the food they eat or the God they pray to. We often find it easier to trust people with whom we share social norms and values. Apparently a person is more likely to employ another person who resembles either themselves or someone they already know and trust. Often our reasons for trusting someone have little to do with them and more to do with a rhyming with our past. If we wish to reach a diverse group potential, in the workplace as well as with our family and friends, we need to cut though unreliable and biased opinions and build our trust on untainted observations. Clichés are just that, we know that not all young blond women are really brainless or all tall white middle-aged men strong and intelligent!

As noted, we become drawn towards the messages we recognise, the ones which make us feel at ease and trust a situation, person, place. Yet, as described in the section: Intuition & Gut [re] Action, we can and do pick up on a wide range of signs. Our senses, if we are consciously receptive to them, can feed us with ample information. For example with our sense of smell: whether it is the smell of the rotting wooden floor beneath our feet, the smell of fear on someone's breath, or mouldy food, stagnant water, gassy air, clean clothes! Each of our five senses contributes to our analysis of whether or not a person or situation is safe: can we trust it, or them, and thrive?

When we consciously combine our 'five sense' perceptions with our experience and knowledge, the kind of trust we establish will be less prone to disappointment. To create, build and maintain trust means we have to see and be seen. Keep asking questions, stay CURIOUS and be flexible enough if necessary to re-assess.

One of the ways to be more astute with believing or not believing is to notice the physical and vocal give-aways which will show when someone is either lying or not to be trusted. In the card game Poker, where part of the game is to convincingly lie, the players are constantly watching their opponents to see if they notice a *'tell'*. This is a minute uncontrollable movement that people make when they are telling a lie. It is amazing when you start to notice this in someone else. Many years ago I was in a legal battle with an ex-colleague. I noticed that each time she was bullshitting or out and out lying, she would make a certain movement with her mouth. It proved a very useful observation! However, it is also useful to double check such repeated *'tells'* as they may not be 100% reliable.

There are different types of trust. We may trust someone's integrity, or we may trust their ability and experience in a certain area. To take the driving example again, when my daughter had just turned eighteen (the legal age to drive in Holland) I would not have trusted her to be able to drive my car, and it would have been illegal for her to do so, since she had not passed her driving test. However, I did trust that she would not try to drive my car until she had passed her test. If we extend this thought into the workplace, you do not always know about people's ability or qualifications. A fundamental belief in their integrity to be open and truthful with you will underpin the relationship. Sometimes the person themselves may not know if they have the capability to do something, and together you may agree to take a calculated risk. This can have inspiring results, and it is often how we grow and explore our potential. Sometimes people do not inform others of their lack of experience or proven ability. If they succeed we may never even know it was in question. But if they do not succeed and we subsequently find out that they did not have the experience and qualification to do the job in hand, then our trust in them will probably diminish. A balance is to decide if it is necessary to explain our position or not.

The ability to disclose will not only come from our own sense of confidence but can be encouraged or discouraged by the degree of trust offered by a group or organisation. In my experience people need to feel safe with another individual or a group of people to have the confidence to admit an area of personal weakness or vulnerability. To build an atmosphere of a *'no blame culture'*, whatever each person's position in the social hierarchy, is a way to achieve this. It can be developed most effectively when mutual respect and appreciation come from the top of an organisation or social structure.

We all make mistakes, it is part of being human. It becomes problematic when we do not trust ourselves or others enough to be able to admit it, or if we do not learn from our past successes and failures.

Trust is generally built up slowly between people. The same goes for building the personal dialogue of trusting ourselves and our own ability to do something. Unfortunately it can all too easily be destroyed in the flash of a moment. This could happen with a small accident like twisting your ankle; you may lose a little trust in your ability to walk without tripping over. It will probably take a day or so to build up your limber-footed ankle-trust again. Trust and experience are interlinked. If we lack trust in our own abilities, then experiences of failure can further undermine our self-trust, and we may become stuck in a downward spiral. This can be reinforced by others around us, particularly if they hold a position of authority. It might be a teacher who undermines a student with their lack of confidence in the student's ability, or a boss who never delegates, constantly micro-manages and only gives negative feedback.

I have noticed that to create and maintain trust within a valued relationship it helps to keep a balance with what we tell and know about each other. It can be a powerful action to disclose your private thoughts, dreams and fears, whatever your position of authority or leadership responsibilities. However, if it remains only one-way traffic, at a certain point the person who has been open and 'trusting' will start to feel too vulnerable and the quality of the relationship will suffer. Conversely, some people use the telling of so-called secrets as a deliberate strategy to elicit trust. Have you ever experienced someone saying to you: *"I am telling you this in confidence, I have never told anyone else"*? You probably felt honoured, trusted, responsible and even valued. Then, if some time later you find out they had in fact told quite a few people, the resulting backlash can make you treat everything that person says or does from then on with scepticism and disbelief. A big GAP in trust is created.

Recently one of my clients, whose main occupation is brokering mergers and acquisitions of large companies, told how in most deals the brilliant concept, graphs and mathematical proof confirming a positive transaction contributes to about only 10% of the making or breaking of a deal. He believes that as much as 90% comes down to interpersonal feeling between the directors of the two companies: *"Do I believe and trust this person enough to proceed with this new business venture?"* These interpersonal feelings of trust come from believing or *'clicking'* with the other person on a gut level. This means that each person needs to be prepared to show themselves and really *'walk the talk'*. This *'walking the talk'* is achieved through making sure your body, voice, imagination and emotions are connecting not only with the content of what you are saying but also skilfully closing the GAP by connecting with the person you are talking with. Many of these communication skills are described in this book.

Few will wholeheartedly follow someone they do not trust.

Trust is never a finished and absolute state. Keep giving yourself the space to re-assess incoming and outgoing messaging. It is not only a wonderful feeling to trust and be trusted, it is also a fundamental component in any interaction. With this ingredient we are more likely to want to spend time together and collaborate. The GAP between us will reduce.

AND-DO-IT
Trust Whos

→ Think of five people who you trust.

→ List about six physical, vocal and behavioural qualities which create that trust.

→ Compare the qualities in each list.

→ With the same people, can you remember any of their past actions or present qualities which may have reduced your trust?

Sometimes distrust comes from a person's long past actions, sometimes from recent actions and sometimes from our own past which has nothing to do with them – can you identify the differences?

AND-DO-IT
Trust Balancing

→ Whenever someone puts emotional or intellectual trust in you, by disclosing personal information, value it and also make sure that it is not only one-way traffic.

→ This does not mean you are obliged to immediately reciprocate your secrets to anyone who wants to tell you theirs. Just keep in mind the balance over the longer time line.

→ Keep an overview of your important relationships, both privately and at work, and make sure the moments of 'putting your trust' in the other person consistently happen and balance both ways.

If you have a position of leadership and responsibility you will regularly have to make strategic decisions concerning the amount of information which needs to be disclosed and to whom, as well as assessing who to trust to do what. Make trust a proactive part of your consideration.

AND-DO-IT

Trust Stretching

In transitory interactions, consider BLIND trust versus DECIDING to trust.

Whilst walking in a busy street or shopping centre:

1. Look at each person as if they are out to get to you – no-one is to be trusted.

2. Look at each person with the attitude: I trust you completely.

3. Look at each person and give yourself a gut reaction grade 1 to 10 concerning how much you trust them.

   Take a moment to see how you arrived at that number. Is there an identifiable pattern to your sense of trusting others when you do not know them?

6 Embracing Ambiguity

This section includes two AND-DO-ITs
...are we lost...

The older we get and the more responsibilities we acquire along the way, the more we are expected to know, give an answer and have a solution, especially if we are in a position of leadership – whether a parent, teacher, medical practitioner, business director or politician.

Our society tries to build an illusion of certainty about the future into its structure in the form of pensions, insurances and predictions. The predictions may be about the stock market, the weather, political events or natural phenomena such as earthquakes. Through these different structures we get pulled into a feeling that we can and should know what will happen. The reality is that although some predictions may be reasonably accurate and helpful, each next second is an educated or wild guess.

If we can dare to regularly be in a place of *'I don't know,'* and even become comfortable with this, it can open up another level of perception and interaction.

When considering figurative and abstract painting, we can expect various strong reactions and preferences. Some people even feel threatened by the ambiguity of an abstract painting. The irony here is that there is plenty of ambiguity in figurative painting as well, but it is a different kind of ambiguity, and may not be identified as such.

I wonder if the beginning of our life has anything to do with an individual's discomfort with ambiguity? When each child is born, as far as we know, it has a purely abstract perception of reality. By creating an abstract, an unidentifiable in an art-form do we re-awaken our fresh young mind? Does the abstract art-form therefore appeal more to those who started life trauma free? Or is our relationship with the abstract, the ambiguous influenced by how the adults around us reacted to our young and flexible thinking?

Hands On

The child draws, paints and shows.
The adult encourages and questions:
"What is it?"
The child explains.
The collection of lines and splodges,
definitely a clear intention.
Both discuss and enjoy.

A few days later the forgetful adult once again
asks the identity of the painting.
The child inspired by change,
gives a completely different answer.
No-one seems to mind,
after all the art critic's article has not been published.

Imagination so often trapped into interpretation, identification.

Can abstract art loosen our perception back to its versatile roots
where we can fly without wings
ride without horses
die and get up again
die and wake up again, and again, and again?

If we dare to not always attempt to classify, box in or have an immediate answer, and even more, if we dare to say: *"I don't know"* (whatever your perceived leadership position happens to be) what do you think could happen? Maybe:

→ More space for collaborative ideas
→ A change of expectations and relationship dynamics
→ Room for others to solve or answer a query

→ Blood pressure reduction
→ Creative out of the box thinking.

It is important to be able to say: *"I don't know"* **without apologising.** It is quite common for people to say: *"I am sorry, I don't know, I cannot answer that question."* This implies that you should apologise for not knowing, that it is something to be ashamed of. Rather than saying: *"No I do not know that writer... book... film... theory, I do not understand what you mean... I do not know how to do this..."*

Creating space and acceptability around the ambiguity of not knowing, whether it is privately within your own mind or publicly by declaring it, can provoke curiosity in both yourself and others. This can move us away from judgemental and defensive interactions.

Time and again when I see executives start to include this dynamic in their communications, both they and their colleagues feel a sense of relief. It is almost too simple to be true! Personally, I have found that the more I admit when I genuinely do not understand or know something the more others around me are happy to help or explain. And sometimes if I declare my confusion other people also admit to not knowing or understanding the same thing. It makes me wonder how many of us are keeping quiet and bluffing understanding. In the competitive political arena or the business world, with the all too often powerful egos involved, is the pull to bluff probable? And what is the impact on effective communication and decision-making? A large GAP in understanding?

If you decide to declare that you do not know something it is useful to **declare this quite quickly**, otherwise you may pass the point of no return. Have you ever answered the phone to hear someone in a warm and friendly voice say for example: *"Hi it's John here..."* or even worse, *"Hi it's me."* Meanwhile you are thinking: *"I know four Johns, which one are you?"* or, *"Who on earth is 'me'?"* It can be hard to ask which John or who is *'me'* as the intimate expectations of the caller can make it feel insulting, insensitive. If I fall into that trap and do not immediately ask, I then spend the next few minutes constructing roundabout questions to try and pin down their identity. But the longer the conversation continues the more impossible it becomes to ask who they are. Similarly in a work context if there is an expectation that you know something and this is not the case, the longer you postpone admitting it, the more tangled the interaction can become.

And yes there are certainly situations where it is useful to pretend certainty. If you are driving late at night, have lost the way and a young frightened child in the back seat of the car asks: *"Are we lost?" "Yes"*, may not be the best way to reply.

Balance the possible outcomes and recognise when to admit to the ambiguity of not knowing and when to bluff, both in your private and professional life.

When used strategically as a tool to engage others, to be ambiguous, resist conclusions and let ideas float can instigate curiosity and engagement. There is a fine line between this and tipping others into feeling irritated and manipulated. Sustaining a positive atmosphere will come from the person leading the discussion remaining genuinely curious towards any possible outcome. In some situations, by defining fewer conclusions, structures and certainties, through ambiguity we can increase collaborative creativity.

Expand the comfort parameters with not knowing, both for yourself and for those around you.

AND-DO-IT
Space Around Not-Knowing

→ If you are in a meeting or situation where you feel you ought to have the answer or know something but in fact you do not, experiment with declaring this...with no apology...

→ Experiment with feeling comfortable with not knowing the answer to something.

→ Suspend any tendencies you may have to jump to conclusions. Keep curious, extend the length of time of not knowing. Notice what happens.

AND-DO-IT
Deconstructing the Language Connection

- → Look at (for example) a tree.
- → Think: this is a tree.
- → This is a branch...this is a leaf...fruit....and so on.

- → Look at the same tree without thinking this is a tree, without thinking what it is at all.
- → Simply see, observe.
- → Each time a thought comes into your mind which defines what you are looking at, let it go.
- → Look and see, without words creating thoughts in your mind.
- → See how long you can sustain observing without categorising and labelling.

- → Repeat looking at the tree and this time imagine this is the first time you have ever seen a tree.
- → See if you can examine the tree with curiosity and maybe even amazement – can you re-create the emotions of a first time experience?

7 Repetition
Does It Exist?

This section contains one AND-DO-IT
...potentially boring...a waste of time...

How often do you have to do the same thing more than once?

From the moment we wake, each day is full of seeming repetition. Some repetition seems unavoidable and is even comforting as it gives a familiar quality to our daily life. For example the pleasure of sitting on the same chair at the dinner table at home, or having the same special cup to drink out of. But some daily actions, for example brushing your teeth, may feel tedious, and you may zone out and think about other things. Repetition can have a tendency to make us anaesthetised towards time-present. But if you were to regularly consider each tooth and feel its size and shape, and the quality of the action, you would probably notice that each time you brushed your teeth, although the action would be categorised as the same action, and therefore repeated, the actual action and experience would always be slightly different.

If you take this idea into each action of your life then repetition does not exist. What do exist are apparently similar actions with subtle differences. It is by revisiting actions over and over again that we learn to do many things, for example to walk, talk, feed ourselves, read, write... The more we experience each time as different the more we will probably learn, and the more sophisticated our actions will become.

If you realise that you can change and vary your perception of any experience, it becomes endlessly fascinating, rewarding and a potential learning curve.

PINK

City
Woman walks
oldish, greyish
topped with a fluffy
clinging pink hat.

Passing

an imposing shop front
dominant colour pink
a brave unusual pink
the same pink.

For a moment

the woman's pink head sinks
into her background
as life matches up too perfectly
she is decapitated.

If we look at the exchange of spoken information, the very words we speak are constantly reused in endless variations and combinations. And there will regularly be a need to repeat the content in one way or another. How may times have you asked someone: "Would you like something to drink?" And what about a chain of meetings where you have to 'repeat' the same message to different groups of people; or when you have to 'repeat' information to someone when you have already explained it once before and they did not understand, or do not remember. Being obliged to re-tell, especially when we believe the other person or people should have understood or listened better, can create quite a negative tension. We may even experience a resistance in ourselves to repair the GAP in understanding, since we feel repetition is an exact re-run and we will gain little from the experience. We numb out. Similarly when we listen to someone repeating the same information or story, as in the case of my darling mother in her later years, it can be hard to remain engaged, interested and interactive.

However, if you become fascinated by the details you will see many differences in any re-run. This makes each interaction much more enjoyable and the quality of your perception will most probably increase exponentially.

A way to sustain alertness with *'repetition'* **is to keep varying and contrasting your focus and perspective.**

Many forms of story-telling use this technique to maintain the attention of the audience. In a film we will be told a story using two main camera shots: the wide-angle long shot and the close-up. If a film is made only of wide-angle long shots, from a distance a view will soon start to appear unchanging. It may become hard for us to remain emotionally connected. With the close-up we will more easily see the subtleties of difference. This information most often appeals directly to our emotional engagement. But if we only see the close-up it will lack context and we may not understand the connection between one shot and another.

Similarly the variation and contrast of the actual camera angle and point of view will add to our ability to see and understand more. We need a balance of many perspectives. The wide shot gives us the context, the close-up gives us the detailed information and more often emotional connection. The combination refreshes our ability to perceive, and gives us a complete and engaging story.

Three 'repeated' versions of the same story

Version 1 – only long shot
Earlier this week there was a massive earthquake in Sumatra. To date the death toll has been put at over 2,000.

Version 2 – only close-up
Ignoring pleas to stop and rest, a Pulau Air resident, Riki, used a broken length of wood to dig at the piles of earth that enveloped the shattered house of a neighbouring family. The bodies of a three-year-old boy and a thirteen-year-old girl had already been taken away. Riki was in Jakarta when the quake struck. *"My family are gone. All of them. I don't know where my mother and father are. And my sister too, she was supposed to get married in one year."*

Version 3 – a combination of the long shot and the close-up
Earlier this week there was a massive earthquake in Sumatra. Ignoring pleas to stop and rest, a Pulau Air resident, Riki, used a broken length of wood to dig at the piles of earth that enveloped the shattered house of a neighbouring family. The bodies of a three-year-old boy and a thirteen-year-old girl had already been taken away. To date the death toll has been put at over 2,000. Riki was in Jakarta when the quake struck. *"My family are gone. All of them. I don't know where my mother and father are. And my sister too, she was supposed to get married in one year."*

A written report like this may capture a reader's imagination, depending on the skill of the writer and the state of mind of the reader. However, if you are saying these words out loud to other people then the accompanying emotion will determine how the hearers join you in the images. **Each time you say the same information you need to re-imagine the pictures behind the words and decide what you feel about them, afresh.** In this way each time you say *'the same thing'* it will be slightly different, fresh, unique.

The choice and combinations of 'wide-angle long shot', 'close-up' and 'camera angle' will vary depending on who you are talking with. With the understanding of these different perspectives it is inspiring to pro-actively tailor the content and the means of communicating your information to suit the character of the group. You can do this if you are aware of the response of the group as you proceed through your message, even if you have told it more than once before. The core ideas remain the same but the dynamics of the content shift with your interactive decisions and relationship.

After all repetition does not exist!

If you hold a leadership position you will probably have many useful experiences which others can learn from. If you re-tell your know-how in this non-repetitive way, others are more likely to learn from your failures and victories. They will be less likely to be compelled to re-invent the wheel.

A way you can apply these approaches if you are predominantly listening, is for example to not only zoom in to the content of what someone is saying, but to also regularly zoom out to see the person who is talking. Become more aware of them in the context of their relationship to everyone else in the room, as well as, for example, their physicality in the space/room at that moment in time.

AND-DO-IT
Perspective Changer

→ Wherever you are sitting, look around you. Notice as much of your visual environment as you can in a few minutes.

→ Now look around, focussing on where you see the colour blue.
→ Now look around the same space, focussing on the colour red.
→ Now look around you noticing where the main source of light is.

→ Notice how the space, information and feelings change as you alter your focus, during this 'repeated' action of looking around you.

8 What & How Do Others Remember What You Have Said

This section includes two AND-DO-ITs

...I felt so disappointed...

How often have you heard someone say: *"I have a great memory..." "I have an awful memory..." "That was memorable...I will never forget what they said"*?

We all have a different memory competence, some of us easily remember dry facts, others situations, people's names, faces, times in our lives, emotions. The memory of facts, perhaps because it appears to be quantifiable, is often seen as the most useful and important. And how often and accurately an individual remembers something very often determines how we assess their intelligence. Information retention will also be tinted with our individual perspective. Do you remember a name as Tom, Tommy, Thomas, Thomas Brown or Mr Brown? How do you remember which name is most appropriate in which situation? When communicating information how can you make sure that others remember the important parts of your message, whatever their individual memory patterns happen to be? And, maybe just as important, that they remember this message represented from your point of view as well as remembering who the information came from?

The ability to do this is useful on several levels:

1. We regularly need to communicate facts and experiences.
2. If your information needs to drive and lead action, then the more everyone remembers, the more unified the resulting group action will be.
3. If a high percentage of person-to-person interaction is accurately understood and remembered, group ideas can creatively develop from a coordinated perspective.
4. If someone remembers the essence of the story and the experience of hearing it, then from whom the story came will

probably spring to mind when they need that expertise. In this way they will know whom to contact if any questions arise.
5. Others can learn from your experience.
6. Time is used efficiently.

So how do I get you to dream my dream? How do I convey information in a way which encourages you to remember something from my point of view? And how do I achieve this, knowing that any communication is a two-way process? How do I also let go of my perspective and prejudices and agree to listen, understand and remember something you have said, from your point of view? The second part of this question is covered in Golden Classics, sections: Giving & Receiving, Levels of Listening – Distracted Versus Focused.

There are clearly ways to imprint ideas and information into someone's mind using brain-washing, bullying, torture or trauma, but I would like to look at how we can achieve this by more pleasurable means.

Throughout history, humans have practised the art of story-telling. We not only enjoy a well-told story but we use it as a tool to exchange, remember information and learn from each other. It is a skilled activity and as such the components are identifiable.

There are two main technical factors that help us to remember someone's story. But before these two components can occur, the teller needs to structure their story in such a way that they mentally revisit the sequence they choose to describe step by step. Then the factors which make the information stick, can come into play. Firstly, if the person is physically and vocally flexible enough, then the spoken imagery will be supported through original and versatile physical and vocal movements. Secondly, if the story-teller re-lives the emotions, the audience through empathy (mirror neuron activity) also experiences the same emotions. In numerous work sessions when checked afterwards to see which bits of concrete information are immediately remembered, it has proved to be the pieces of information which are communicated with these two qualities. We remember:

1. The information which is supported by physicality and vocal expression in line with the imagery.

2. The information which the story-teller gives whilst re-experiencing the appropriate emotion(s). It is the difference between saying: *"I felt so disappointed"* and actually re-feeling the disappointment as you recount the events. The re-experiencing is the quality whereby your information is more likely to imprint into the hearer's emotional experience and be remembered.

To help define and activate point 2, the emotion part in this, we can work with three primary human emotions. This approach is particularly relevant within a business context where so often people feel that to communicate with emotions is unacceptable. Being *'emotional'* may be perceived as being emotionally out of control and therefore not business-like. By identifying and accessing three primary human emotions we create a clear emotion-anchor with which to underpin any conversation, however emotionally barren the context or content happens to be.

Empathy:
People need to regularly feel that you can appreciate and understand them from their point of view. By doing this you acknowledge them. They will be more likely to be open to you, be able to absorb different ideas and remember you.

Decisiveness:
Most conversations need moments of clarity and decision-making, otherwise they go round in endless circles of discussion. This emotion is a feeling of conviction whereby you have no need to convince anyone.

It is simply you stating with ease and confidence your belief or need at that moment. It may be something as simple as stating: *"I want that report on my desk tomorrow morning."* It is an emotion to create clarity of understanding and action.

Enthusiasm:
This is a motivator. For people to feel passionate and excited about what they are doing or what they could do will inspire them to tackle all kinds of situations, developments and ideas with desire, energy and pleasure.

Of course people experience many shades and combinations of these three emotions plus numerous others. However, if we make sure that we are continually balancing and using these three emotions in any exchange, then the basic essentials will be covered.

Home emotions
The majority of people I have met and worked with tend to have a *'home emotion'*. By this I mean that most of the time they are pulled towards one over-riding emotion. This will generally be the emotion which has received the most positive reinforcement from their environment. So if we use the above categories individuals will frequently be either:
→   The really good listener and empathetic type.
→   The focussed decisive type.
→   The ever-positive up-tempo enthusiastic type.

Because the *'home emotion'* is so familiar and comfortable, the danger is overuse, leading to the strength becoming a weakness.

Whilst it is useful to have mastered one home emotion, having a clear and strong grasp on all three core emotions, and knowing when, where, and how to use them, is fundamental for a number of reasons. Contrast and juxtaposition of emotion helps us to feel and re-feel the depth of the matter in hand. It also makes the information stick. Overuse of one emotion can lead listeners to blank out or even feel distracted and tired. In these cases the effective exchange and remembering of information is significantly reduced.

There are many interactions which can also lull us into staying in one emotion. It is all too easy to get pulled into the initial most obvious and perhaps dominant emotion of a given situation, even when we try to do otherwise. Maybe this is why, at funerals, although we may try, with the content of what we say, to celebrate the dead person's life, it is all too easy to become overwhelmed by grief. As you describe the deceased, if you really re-visit some joyful, happy occasions in their life, then the enormity of them no longer being alive will become more profound, three-dimensional, vivid.

Another type of one-emotion contact which we can easily be pulled into, is replying to someone in the same emotion as the one they have just given. Particularly if that emotion is a strong one, such as anger. If this happens it is then hard for the conversation to move past that point, and effective communication is unlikely.

Juxtaposition and change of emotions will lead to a fuller, more memorable description of information or proposed course of action. It will also stimulate interaction. If we strategically change emotion during an interaction/conversation the actual thinking and content is more likely to progress in an interesting, memorable and creative way.

Since most of us are increasingly swamped with information, having the ability to be unforgettable is more important than ever. Businesses have long known this, and are regularly prepared to make large investments in their marketing and advertising, but learning the precise communication skills for individual company members to be memorable has had less attention or budget.

A defining factor inspiring a colleague or client to choose an idea, product or collaboration will be if you and your ideas spring into their mind and stick there when they are making those decisions.

AND-DO-IT

The Three Core Emotions

→ Use the three core emotions in one chosen conversation.

→ Make sure that you use them several times, sometimes for a moment, sometimes for longer.

→ Check later to see what has been remembered. Possibly see if the receiver has noticed your emotional shifts.

→ Try using and sticking to one of the core emotions for a whole conversation/meeting and notice what happens or does not happen, and what is or is not remembered.

Repeat the above exercise:
→ This time focus on pro-actively using your body (arms, shoulders, head position, face…) and voice to support the chosen emotion.

→ Another time try keeping physically rigid with no vocal modulation with the chosen emotion. It may prove surprisingly hard to do this. Once again check later to see what has been remembered.

AND-DO-IT
The Story-Telling Building Blocks

For a story or spoken communication to effectively resonate, use the following techniques:

1. 'Believe' the contents.

2. Actively imagine the moment-to-moment imagery.

3. Re-live each emotion (what do you feel at that moment) as you re-tell the content. Strategically make sure all three core emotions are regularly used.

4. Include physical and vocal awareness and dexterity.

5. Be sensitive to the audience and adjust the pace of the delivery and quantity of information to correspond to their needs.

6. Juxtapose different perspectives: close-up/long shot/wide-angle.

7. Begin and end with clarity, sensitivity and commitment.

Try using some or all of these seven elements whenever you have the mental space to include them.

9 Strategic Emotion

This section includes one AND-DO-IT
...fear of the man eating Miranda...

Part of each person's relationship with the rest of the world consists of an emotional interaction. We experience emotions all the time whether we like it or not. It is unstoppable. We share this quality with many animals. And like them, part of our survival mechanism is to sense one another's emotions. What can get confusing is that, unlike animals, we also spend quite some time hiding or at least trying to hide what we are feeling. We do this for a mountain of reasons usually developed during the civilising process. For example, if a young child is given a toy which they do not like, the child will probably show their disappointment clearly. This will continue until adults train the child to smile gracefully and strategically thank the giver for the *"oh so lovely present"*. Can you think of examples from your childhood when you were encouraged to alter your emotional response to something? We are taught that trying to suppress our emotions will ease interactions so we can peaceably live together. On a daily basis there will probably be many moments ranging from trivial to significant when each one of us strategically adjusts our emotions.

If someone is saying one thing and feeling another deep down, we tend not to really believe them. Often we will not know why, not be able to quite put our finger on it, but we feel a fundamental distrust. Apart from the factor of *'attempting to hide or disguise a feeling'* another element which can confuse is that we may be experiencing several feelings at the same time. If you walk into a room full of people, there may be some you like, admire, are intimidated by, bored by, curious about... and you will experience all these contradictory emotions jumbled up together. People feel uncertain and insecure when they see inconsistency between someone else's emotion and their spoken word. Conversely, when a person's emotions are aligned with what they are saying, they appear wonderfully clear and trustworthy. We will probably recognise both these extremes in ourselves as well as with our friends, family members and colleagues. With the people we know well, we often catch on faster when there is a discrepancy between their feelings and what they are actually saying and doing. In which case we may then question them further to find out what they are really meaning or feeling.

If our own emotions and actions are in harmony the feel-good factor will probably increase. In turn a fundamental ease will radiate from us even if the message we have to give is a hard one. To interact with someone who is in emotional balance with what they are saying is captivating.

To spend most of our time in situations where our function and feelings are in tune with each other is probably what most of us will hope for. The daily reality often unfolds differently. There will be many moments of varying importance when we experience a GAP in this. It could be something as small as meeting someone who asks: *"How are you?"* and you immediately say: *"Fine thanks,"* when in reality you have a headache. Intuitively they will notice the GAP and a moment of doubt occurs.

How can we remain in line with whatever we are feeling, while doing whatever is required of us in our daily interactions? How can we maintain integrity of emotion when we have to work or socialise with people who given the choice we would not spend much time with? Or when we work for a company whose policy cannot be 100% in line with how we feel all of the time? How can we change emotionally grating situations into something dynamic and fascinating and at the same time not short-change our own emotional household?

As noted, human beings can do something with their emotions, which as far as we know, animals cannot do. We do not simply react emotionally to one another in an instinctive and automatic way. Through our imagination we can change the way we actually feel. Not everyone is aware of having this ability, but it is something that can be learned. When used with awareness and pro-active skill it can transform any interaction, however uncomfortable or stuck it may be.

To immediately identify this process, choose someone you love and remember a specific thing that they recently did which made you smile.

Wait until you can see this in your mind's eye and wait until you start to feel the sensation of this emotion related to that memory...............

Now stop thinking about them and replace the image with someone who you find irritating or annoying. Think specifically of something they have recently done which has had a negative impact on you............

Wait until you start to feel the emotion related to this memory..........

Did you experience two different feelings happening even throughout your body? Both emotions were genuine. You re-created them through thinking back to a specific occasion.

There are regularly situations when personal feelings can have a confusing or negative impact. For example, part of your job may be to collaborate with someone you do not particularly like. If you do not change that underlying feeling of dislike it will sabotage any mutual understanding. They will sense it.

Another recognisable dynamic is when a strong feeling leaks from one situation into another. You may be in a meeting in which you feel annoyed. If you do not do something about that, it is likely to stay with you and leak into the next meeting. This could result in the people in the second meeting misinterpreting your annoyance and perhaps even taking it personally as your underlying irritation may not fit with the words you are saying. The UNDERSTANDING GAP increases and may even continue to increase with the possible frustrations of not being understood by both sides. This may then have to be followed by a damage-repair meeting where you have to re-explain yourself and your intentions. A regular initial reaction to this concept is: *"No, no! This is acting, I just want to be my authentic self."* This response may come from the fear of appearing artificial, fake. I am sure we have all experienced the phoney emotion which has been thrust upon us by someone who is trying to convince or motivate us to accept them and their ideas. It often has a repellent effect as we clearly sense their insincerity. In this context sometimes the word *'acting'* is used as a pejorative to describe insincerity.

Actors study for years to learn the techniques to convincingly portray someone else. One of the elements in this study is to learn how to change personal emotions at will, in a believable and authentic way. This is also a useful skill for anyone in a leadership position. The actor then takes this expertise, along with many others, several steps further. Their profession is to believably portray another human being in the context of a written, usually fixed, text: the play or film script.

The Ferdinand story

One of the productions I acted in with the Pip Simmons Theatre Group was our version of Shakespeare's The Tempest. The one story line in the play which I found the least interesting was the love element between the young prince Ferdinand and Miranda. So when Pip, the director, cast me as the young prince I was disappointed and annoyed. Knowing how important it is in the theatre to be a team player, I nonetheless applied myself to my part in the production. I learnt to play the trombone for an initial trombone trio, to herald our shipwrecked arrival on the mysterious island. I spent most of the production with a large plank of wood strapped to my back, and the rest of the time I only had eyes for Miranda. Or at least that was what I tried to do. But I kept questioning why Pip had asked me, a woman, to play this young prince, who for the entire play was in love with Miranda. BORING! I tried all kinds of approaches, imagining this and that along the way. After each performance, Pip would come backstage and give the actors some director's notes: "*Do this... try that*". But they never really shifted my underlying struggle with the original casting. I was doing my best to give a professional performance. Sometimes my choices worked well, sometimes they did not, and I could never quite identify why. I felt as if I was stumbling around in the dark.

Then one evening during the show I had an epiphany! I realised that Pip's casting was brilliant. Ferdinand, who had had little exposure to young women until this point in his life, had fallen desperately in love with the gorgeous, self-confident Miranda. He wanted to be with her, talk with her, kiss her and touch her. But he had no sexual experience and did not know what to do, how to do it... where to start. I realised I could identify exactly the same feelings within myself. I was heterosexual and had never touched another woman's breast or kissed a woman in a sexual way, but I knew what it was like to fall desperately in love. I realised if I combined those two very real personal experiences I would come pretty close to how Ferdinand might be feeling, and therefore behaving. For the rest of the production, by paralleling these particular combinations of my own experience, together with Shakespeare's words, I was able to portray Ferdinand in an authentic, touching and humorous way. As I recognised these elements within myself and empathised with the character Ferdinand, the audience could in turn empathise with me playing Ferdinand. This resulted in my portrayal of Ferdinand being recognised as: '*Jessie Gordon's all-female Ferdinand, who with her tensely-comic fear of the man eating Miranda and her fluttering sexually confused half gesture was just about as perfect as could be.*' Plays and Players, July 1978

Up until then acting had been a hit and miss experience for me. But from that moment I understood how to access the emotional building blocks involved in the process of acting, and how to do this on a consistent and inspiring level. That evening when Pip came backstage he just looked at me, nodded and smiled, and I smiled and nodded back. We knew, and now I finally understood the art of acting and felt for the first time I could legitimately call myself an actress.

It also became clear what the difference was between acting and being a consistently inspiring communicator. The actor uses their imagination and emotional memory to pluck a certain cocktail from their own experience to re-create the main elements of the character they are portraying. The successful communicator connects to their content and to the people they are talking with so that their feelings are in line with what they are saying, from a personal point of view, and also in line with the audience. If for whatever reason their feelings become disconnected with one or more of these elements, they will immediately realise it and have the skills to re-engage using their library of emotional memories.

There is a crucial difference between doing and being. It is when someone pretends or 'does' an emotion that we feel they are phoney and insincere. When someone actually lives or re-lives an emotion we in turn will feel it, believe it and understand them.

Using this pro-actively is a core leadership skill.

To give a simple example: during a meeting, I am leading a discussion and feeling empathetic to everyone in the group. Continuing with this empathetic feeling and tone I say: *"Interesting discussion everyone. Thank you for all your contributions. I would like to remind you all that in five minutes, by the end of this meeting, we all need to come to a decision, make a choice."* My empathy, which understands everyone's point of view including perhaps two people who would prefer to make the decision tomorrow, underpins the whole statement. Because of this it may be hard for the two doubters to really believe my request that they let go of their needs and be motivated to make the choice. They will be inspired by my empathetic tone to continue discussing. If instead, to lead and inspire their thinking to move on, I say the second part with a feeling of clarity and decision: *"By the end of this meeting, we all need to come to a decision, make a choice,"* they will be emotionally motivated to really hear and accept this request and choose accordingly.

A leader who exercises the skill of strategically changing their emotion, will be more likely to effectively guide and motivate discussions and decision-making.

AND-DO-IT
Changing Authentic Emotion

In between one interaction and another experiment with the following four steps:

1. Recognise your current main feeling. If the emotion is in tune with your current interaction, then stay with it. If not, 'park it'. Try parking it by doing a small physical action (such as wriggling your toes) to bring your attention back into 'time present'. Or for example notice and focus on a specific detail of something around you (a smell, sound, taste, colour...) for a few seconds.

2. By **engaging in your imagination coupled with a clear emotional memory** bring in another very real feeling. This can either be related to the people or person you are with or about to meet, or related to something from your past. For example, if you want to be genuinely enthusiastic towards that person/group and you cannot at that moment feel it, **then think back to a clear, defined time in your life when you have felt enthusiasm**.

3. Keep building on that image until you start to re-experience the feeling in your body.

4. Once that feeling is established, meet with the person/people in question.

When you get used to directing your emotions in this way you can use this tool in meetings on a moment-to-moment basis.

Using the three core emotions described in the section: What & How Do Others Remember What You Have Said, you can strategically lead the emotional and thinking atmosphere.

10 Distance & Intimacy

This section includes one AND-DO-IT
...I am human too...

Each relationship interaction will have changing variations of intimacy and distance. Some of the feelings of intimacy are two way and very real, and some may be an illusion. For example, when we see a public figure being interviewed on television, or an actor in a movie, it can provoke quite a strong fake feeling that we intimately know them. This could come from recognising detailed close-ups of the movement of their mouth, or an emotion expressed on their face. The illusion of intimacy can also happen when we are profoundly moved by the work of a writer, visual artist, musician or composer. The disjointed feeling of simultaneous intimacy and distance particularly struck me when the Dutch visual artist and poet Lucebert died in 1994.

Thank you in air

Lucebert.
We shared a time together, being alive.
I knew of you.
Your ideas have affected and tickled my mind.

Yet you knew nothing of me.

That strange lop-sided relationship
the famous with their public.
I feel a rush of sadness that we never met.
Although I had countless encounters with your artistry
I never dared to make the step to search you out.
In some unreasonable way, I feel you have abandoned me.

And knowing that a few days ago you left for good
I have an urge to run to the bookcase

pull out a catalogue and remind myself.
Touch the body of your work.
The work which no doubt art galleries
will now re-calculate
into a good buy.

This kind of imbalance can also happen in the workplace. Most company employees will know what their CEO and the members of the managing board look like and be aware of these people's ideas and company policies. But the CEO and managing board in a large company cannot possibly have a similar knowledge about everyone who works for them. This disparity with distance and intimacy can become quite uncomfortable if the person in a leadership position does not realise or have the skills to elegantly guide the dynamics. There are meeting structures which can help, from the formal, distant boardroom and conference set-up to the informal, more intimate working lunch, or conversation over coffee. Intimacy seems to happen more when we eat or drink together. But whatever the social or structural context it is useful to be able to guide the dynamic in such a way that each person present clearly understands. I have noticed that this is a regular topic of discussion and concern. If a director has developed a chummy repartee with an employee in one situation, it can be hard to change to a more distant relationship in another context without causing offence. If the director feels uncomfortable, they may be clumsy and blunt. However, if handled well, the switch back and forth can be fun. For example, in a more official context the handshake could easily establish an appropriate distance and a warm smile could acknowledge an earlier less formal discussion.

Funnily enough, when we meet someone moments of intimacy are not necessarily reliant on having concrete information about that person. Have you ever felt an intimate click with someone without knowing anything about them? It could come from a certain look in their eyes, a subtle smell or physical movement. Conversely, do you know people with whom you feel distant and unconnected, even after exchanging plenty of information with them? A click can happen with shared interests, beliefs, cultural reference points, political affiliations, humour. And even if these qualities are not shared, you may feel an inexplicable curiosity to learn more about that person. Or on learning more about someone you may feel inspired to make more distance between you! However, we sometimes need to put aside our personal preferences and skilfully close the GAP in order to work with someone productively.

Projecting the image of *'I am human too'* can create a feeling of intimacy with large groups of people. Precise physical touch which is purposefully placed before the camera can achieve this.

A much-used technique which does not need too much homework or information is the *'kissing the baby gesture,'* popular amongst British politicians during election campaigns. The power of displaying physical touch is also sometimes used by famous people who are trying to bring worldwide attention to the plight of the disadvantaged. The closer they are seen to be, the more they touch the war victim or the starving person – filmed in close-up – the more potent the message seems to become. In 1987 Princess Diana visited Aids patients and held their hands, touched them physically. At the time, people were ignorant and fearful about how contagious an Aids patient could be, and her small but significant actions of public physical intimacy proved to have a powerful effect. They cut across the distance caused by prejudice and stigma.

When touch is agreed on by both parties, it can create intimacy. The reverse also holds true: if the recipient dislikes it, it can increase the feeling of distance. The message of intimacy or distance created with the action of touching another person is subtle and can be powerful when used with sensitivity.

From our birth we all need to be touched, it is vital to healthy development and continuing well-being. As we get older, depending on the culture, sets of rules shape us into using certain acceptable patterns of *'touch'* behaviour. If touch has an insincere or predatory motive, unless the receiver is lonely and affection-starved, they will feel it immediately, in which case the action will probably create emotional distance. In many western countries it is more common for women to feel comfortable with touching other people than it is for men. Unfortunately touch between men is often only acceptable in a context of sport or heavy drinking bouts. In the workplace, due to the fear of being accused of sexual harassment, many men have been pushed into the extreme of no physical contact. This can reduce their repertoire in the often subtle area of distance and intimacy.

How we look at one another can also have an effect on feelings of distance and intimacy.

If someone looks with a certain emotion the change from distance to intimacy can be instant. We will often be particularly sensitive to the look in the eyes of people we love, know well, dislike or fear. Conversely, avoiding eye contact creates distance. It can give a strange contradictory message when someone's voice, words and gesture profess a pleasure to be with you and yet they give you little or no eye contact. This may be simple shyness, or it may be the person who greets you with a warm shake of the hand, whilst simultaneously scanning the room with their eyes to see who else they may wish to meet.

The tone of our voice is another tool which can direct the supple ebb and flow with these dynamics.

Quick call story

The telephone rang in my office. I answered it and a voice with a mid-European accent said: *"Hello, this is Mischa here."* For a few seconds I forgot that earlier in the day I had emailed an interested client called Mischa and that this would in all probability be him ringing me back. My immediate response was: how amazing, my cousin from Austria who I have not talked with for ages is ringing me up. My voice was full of warmth and delight as I said: *"Oh Mischa hello!"* Then within a split second I realised who it was and we continued our business conversation. However, the warmth and intimacy in my first few words resulted in him also responding in an exceptionally warm and interested way. A powerful closeness was created by the tone in my voice.

These tones are easy to pick up on through the telephone. Have you ever rung a number needing some help or advice and the person on the other end of the phone, in a distant, bored voice, says: *"Hello can I help you?"* Clearly the most useful next action would be to put the phone down! A great deal of global business is now done over the phone, often in the structure of conference calls. An ability to change the tone and intimacy in your voice will have a great deal of influence on the outcome of such exchanges.

If you are a newcomer in a group of friends or colleagues who know each other well, you may feel distant, excluded. I recently had a client who had been promoted from outside a division to lead a team of five people who were *'best friends'*. For some reason the group, who had an intimate and easy repartee with each other, were not interested or willing to let him in. He in turn, in his role as their boss, maintained a distance. Over a period of about a year there was little shift in these first dynamics, resulting in a lack of connection from all sides. And although the department was achieving top results on a financial level, the entire team finally cast a vote of no confidence in his leadership. He was innovative and talented, but because he did not have the skills to create intimacy with his team, and perhaps realised too late how important it was, he never gained their respect, empathy or trust. His division director did not support him and he was asked to step down. He subsequently decided to leave, so the company lost an asset and he through this painful learning curve lost a job.

It is in everyone's interest that we vary the distance and intimacy dynamics so that our range of collaborative understanding is well rounded.

On a practical day-to-day level where all kinds of actions need to be instigated, juxtaposing the two qualities can help to clarify our decision-making process. We often need to step back for a moment before making a decision. After which, if we then easily change to more intimacy with genuine warmth, the conversation can progress to the next issue. This is quite easy to recognise in the role of parenting. On a regular basis children need warmth, affection and intimate understanding, but if the parents cannot change their emotional tone to create a distance when, for example, they need the child to take a dangerous situation more seriously, then the child will suffer. It will have a less developed, perhaps naive understanding of the world and be hindered in its ability to survive, let alone thrive.

Our use of names for each other is another simple yet powerful way to set up the tone of a conversation and create intimacy or distance. For example, if my daughter called me Ms Gordon, or my doctor called me Darling, it would throw the accepted dynamics off kilter. Sometimes people talk about a politician or other important person using only their first name, as a statement of intimacy. And some people suggest intimacy with claiming statements such as: *"Oh that is typically you...I would never have expected that from him...you of all people...I love that about her...I know you would never do that...I can always trust you to say what you think..."*

There will always be moments when it is useful to change the dynamics of intimacy and distance consciously during an interaction. It can have a profound effect on individual relationships as well as on a group's power structure.

AND-DO-IT
Changing the D & I

Notice during a telephone conversation how the feeling of distance and intimacy may change.
See what you can do to alter the dynamics by experimenting with some of the following:

→   Use longer sounds: instead of a clipped *"Yes"* (impatience and distance) as you listen, make it a longer *"Yeeees"* (interest and intimacy).

→   Make no sound at all as the other person is talking and wait a few beats before replying (distance).

→   Change the speed of talking – talking quite a few grades faster or slower than your innate tempo.

→   Change your thoughts about the other person as you talk. For example, focus on a quality you find annoying, and then focus on a quality you find sympathetic.

→   Talk as if you have all the time in the world.

→   Talk as if you have little time and too much to do.

11 Inclusion & Exclusion

This section includes four AND-DO-ITs
...perhaps Betty or Hugh...

Society is made up of different groups, which by definition include some and exclude others. Historically our survival has relied on being accepted in a particular group, so we can have quite deep feelings about being included or excluded. To this day many political conflicts pivot round the concept of one group versus another. This inclusion/exclusion dynamic also resonates into all kinds of daily interactions. This could be manifested in the smallest movement: someone turning slightly away from you, literally giving you the cold shoulder, an insincere voice, a roll of the eyes or someone standing a bit too close, asking inappropriate questions, staring... Being part of one group or another will regularly be shifting its emphasis and importance. How can we balance the realistic practicality of being included or excluded in a certain group, with the confusing or even contradictory emotions sometimes ignited by these changes? Children can be surprisingly cruel in the way they push a *'friend'* out of their group one minute and then include them the next. Most of us will probably have experienced this from our earliest youth and will have residue emotional memories which can get re-triggered later on in our life. It is useful to be aware of these different feelings and decide how important they are.

To be an outsider is not necessarily negative, it can sometimes give us the freedom to take inspiring risks.

Cartoon story

When I first moved to live in Holland I was in the process of also changing from the acting profession to becoming a full time visual artist and illustrator. I had no formal training but was inspired and encouraged by a few professional artists. My portfolio was full of rather inexperienced, primitive drawings. Nevertheless I found out the names and addresses of the main newspapers and magazines, and made the rounds. One of the newspapers I visited was a weekend newspaper called *Vrij Nederland*. I am not sure if I would have had the cheek and confidence to visit a newspaper of equivalent historical weight in England, but in Holland this paper had no emotional connection for me. So with the confidence of an outsider I strode into their head office and announced that they needed to have a weekly cartoon strip and I was the person to do it. To my amazement they said OK and gave me a six-week assignment. I had never made a cartoon strip in my life. My drawings, although humorous, were always one-frame comments. I went home, struggled, sweated and managed to fulfil the commission. All six cartoon strips were published and my career as a cartoonist/illustrator progressed.

I believe one of the reasons I transmitted enough confidence to receive the commission was because my sense of well-being did not relate to or depend on this institution. It was not riding on whether I was accepted and included, or rejected and therefore excluded. I had deliberately not found out the importance of the newspaper, and was therefore not in awe of either the institution or the people in it. In this case, ignorance was bliss! I walked through the door with curiosity and an *"I can do it"* attitude.

It is one thing to choose to be an outsider or to be included in a group but quite another experience if the group itself *'lets you in'* or *'keeps you out'*. If you experience being excluded from a group for reasons which make sense to you and which you agree with all well and good. But if the exclusion is malicious, confusing or destructive it is probably useful to do something about it. That could be by simply 'walking away' or if it is important to be included then assess who within the group would be the best person to discuss this with. Before discussing it is useful to consciously 'park' any feelings of resentment or hurt. The **AND-DO-IT**: Perception Bouncing – Situations, in section: Past . Present . Future, will help with this. Sometimes inclusion is not as important as it may feel. Keeping alert to the importance of an occasion and the function of a particular group can help keep the deep desire to be included or even excluded in perspective.

If we develop the abilities to individually choose inclusion, whilst not fearing rejection, we can gain an independence to creatively explore.

The individual make-up of a group and each person's sense of belonging is sometimes crucial to the success of the group action. If a team of doctors and nurses in an operating theatre were not being inclusive by communicating and connecting well with each other, would you want to be their patient? Something as simple as a medical team knowing each other's names before surgery starts can strikingly reduce error percentage, as described in Dr Atul Gawande's insightful book *The Checklist Manifesto*.

If we consider our body with all the different functions working in harmony together it can be seen as an inspiring model for inclusive group behaviour. If for whatever reason we exclude a part of our body, after awhile we will most likely become ill. To discount the contribution of any bodily functions on purpose would be ridiculous.

TOE

> How would you know
> If your toe
> was to grow?
> Grow and know
> that the toe
> which started so
> well,
> so
> pretty and group like,
> a part of the foot

a collective,
supportive.
How would you know
that the toe
had said NO.
A solo career
not just one of the ten,
not the left or the right,
middle, big, small or other.
But a life with a name,
perhaps Betty or Hugh
and a house not a shoe...
I suppose you would know
for the toe
it would go.

In our society, we put a lot of focus on celebrating the individual, regardless of their leadership capabilities. Many cultures regularly put people on pedestals, making them almost superhuman. *"No-one else could have done that, they are unique, and they did it by themselves..."* Consider a few icons of the past 100 years: Albert Einstein, Nelson Mandela, Marilyn Monroe and Michael Jackson. Einstein could not have arrived at his ideas without the ideas of others preceding and around him. Nelson Mandela could not have survived his years in prison without the support of his friends, family and colleagues, and he might never have been released without the years of worldwide protest and trade sanctions. And Marilyn Monroe, she was an icon of what? Was it beauty and success, or addiction and loneliness? Then most recently the tragedy of what individual recognition did to Michael Jackson. Did the expectation and desire of the masses push this talented individual into the macabre extremes of the behaviour we witnessed in his latter years? This kind of fanatical adoration damages not only the individual but also society, as people strive to emulate such role models.

If we juxtapose this movement towards individualism with society's insistence that we all conform, then the two messages can feel extreme and contradictory. We are all too often encouraged to be 'normal' – a considerate contributing part of the group – and 'unique' – a special individual, separated from the group – at the same time.

Another dynamic at play is that our society designates particular inclusive or exclusive roles to group members which are connected to qualities beyond our control, such as gender, age and race. With the following list notice which gender, age and ethnicity immediately spring to mind:
→ A nurse in a hospital in London, giving a patient a bed bath.
→ A director chairing a meeting in a large office in New York.
→ A parent feeding their children at home.
→ Leaders of ten countries lining up for a photo shoot.
→ A teacher teaching a class of six-year-olds in a school in Europe.
→ A lecturer teaching mathematics to university students in Africa.
→ Firefighters entering a burning building.
→ Six ballet dancers, dancing on stage.
→ Builders constructing an office block.

It is impossible not to have pre-conceived notions about people, including a certain type of person in one particular group, or excluding them from another. Even after all the changes related to gender at work, I still hear how women directors get taken for the assistant, particularly if their assistant happens to be male. It is interesting to experiment with challenging one's own presumptions about these stereotypes and notice how this can change another person's sense of inclusion and exclusion. The UNDERSTANDING GAP will shift.

Walking past a construction site in London recently, my attention was taken by the following sign:

DANGER MEN WORKING OVERHEAD

I smiled at the thought of changing the sign to

DANGER WOMEN WORKING OVERHEAD	or	DANGER PEOPLE WORKING OVERHEAD

In any interaction you may want to actively include someone, for example making someone feel welcome. Or actively exclude someone, for example preventing a destructive group member from dominating a meeting. The active use of some of the communication skills listed in the AND-DO-ITs can enhance the overall motivation and cohesion of a group.

AND-DO-IT
Eyes - Body - Voice

Group or one on one
1. Eyes

→ Next time you are talking to a group, keep including everyone with your eye contact. Be particularly aware that if one person asks a question you need to give the reply to the whole group.

→ Vary the length of time and intensity of your looking at individuals. At a certain point the person may stop feeling included and begin to feel you are staring and therefore excluding them.

→ Notice if someone is not mentally participating. Give them extra eye attention!

→ During the next few days notice how you can include or exclude others in a conversation, by either looking or not looking at them.

2. Physical positioning
Make sure that you are not blocking people from being able to have contact with each other.

→ Sitting – consider sitting further away from the edge of the table so people either side of you can also see each other, have contact.

→ Standing – with a small group keep widening the circle if others join the group.

→ Standing – in front of a large group make sure that everyone is easily within your circle of vision.

→ Change your position from time to time. This will change your spatial relationship with everyone in the room, so if you have been excluding someone by mistake, you are more likely to notice and start including them again.

3. Voice
In Golden Classics see the section: Our Voice, which discusses the difference between pushing and flowing sound.

AND-DO-IT
Old Hurt or New

→ If you experience a strong emotion connected to being included or excluded from a certain group, take a moment to think about it.

→ Note if your reaction is related to an old hurt, or if it is to do with the situation which is actually happening. Being aware of this difference can help you to decide how to cope with it.

AND-DO-IT
Choosing In or Out

→ Identify one social group which you choose to exclude yourself from. Note one action you take to bring this about.

→ Identify one social group which you choose to include yourself in. Note one action you take to bring this about.

AND-DO-IT
Checking Connections

→ When talking with a group consider pivotal elements you have in common as well as possible differences.

→ Adjust the conversation to include the reference points you share.

→ If you are unsure, ask the question, even if it seems obvious. For example:
Has everyone had access to the same information, report, book, film... ?
Has everyone shared the same experience: visited a certain country, worked with a certain person...?
Does everyone know what you mean with a generic term?
Keep noticing if your interpretation of 'normal', 'nice', 'funny', 'tragic'... is the same as theirs.

→ See and hear the qualities of the replies, not just the content. In this way you will get a feeling of how included or excluded someone may be feeling.

12 Diversity & Decision-Making

This section includes one AND-DO-IT
...unable to prevent self-interest...

Happily, we live in a world full of human variety. But our reactions to the different people around us can be extreme, ranging from delight and fascination to fear and aggression. As worldwide interaction grows between a greater diversity of people, in turn the differences between us become increasingly important in the communication equation. In corporate life the need to pro-actively facilitate a balanced diversity is being placed higher on the agenda. It is also becoming harder for the majority to accept that those in power do not reflect the diversity of their society.

To the question: *"Does the variety of members in our governments and corporate governance truly reflect the society they are representing?"* can be added: *"Does the classroom mix in our schools give the next generation a typical cultural blend and hands-on experience of the society they will inherit?"* and *"Is there across-the-board access to power and education?"* The answer to all three questions is more often than not, no.

Diversity in a country's population will be shown in the differences of age, gender, race, income and wealth, intellect, religion, health and nationality. These categories will also experience different forms of discrimination. Depending on the requirements and aims of any particular organisation a certain cocktail of diversity will be favoured. Sometimes a lack of diversity in an institution is pro-actively chosen for seemingly good reasons: for example, an old people's home will have 100% old people as the resident population. But even then the ethics behind putting elderly people all together in one institution and for example children all together in another are worth re-evaluating.

Certain businesses and products will also attract a specific customer. For example, clearly a shop selling fashionable clothes for young people, if successful, will have a majority buying-population of young people! If we then consider the business model for this, would the shop favour a young manager and fashion buyer and would this preference lead to the success of the business? Alternatively would it be wiser to employ someone older with more business experience, or would the winning team be diverse and include both? Logically to include a useful spread of qualities and experience in a managerial team means there can be a wide range of knowledge and diverse approaches to problem solving. And yet this model is not used as often as it could be.

With corporate and political governance it can be time consuming and complex to come up with an estimate for a representational balance of people. But one category, which can be calculated with a click of the computer keys and is blatantly obvious, is the gender mix. In 2010, one global analysis of the sex ratio noted 986 females per 1,000 males and trended to reduce to 984 in 2011. So just under 50% of the population worldwide is female. Anyone can see that this is not reflected even slightly by the percentage of women holding decision-making positions, outside the home. Inside the home the power balance is more subtle and individual.

In recent years, discussion of diversity has focussed mainly on women, and particularly the lack of women holding professional leadership positions – maybe because this is so easy to identify. Sometimes the word sexism is also used, but I have noticed that when I use the word sexism many people feel uncomfortable and more often than not will avoid using it. Are they uncomfortable about the word because they feel uncomfortable about the subject?

Dictionary definition:
Sexism
Also known as **gender discrimination** *or* **sex discrimination***, is the application of the belief or attitude that there are characteristics implicit to one's gender that indirectly affect one's abilities in unrelated areas.*

It is a form of discrimination or devaluation based on a person's sex, with such attitudes being based on beliefs in traditional stereotypes of gender roles. The term sexism is most often used in relation to discrimination against women but can apply to both sexes.

When I ask different groups of professional women if anyone has experienced sexism in the workplace, it is often hotly denied, particularly by the younger women. I will never forget the time when a young female executive then went on to eulogise her boss, saying how just and kind he was. To illustrate her point she explained that after working for him for three years she found out she was not being paid the same amount as her male counterpart. When she questioned this inequality she was struck by how surprised her boss was and that he instantly raised her salary to be in line with her colleague. She believed his sympathy and immediate response confirmed his unbiased leadership. I then asked her if... *"surely as part of his responsibility, would not her boss participate in the yearly discussion concerning his team's salaries?"* Her smile melted away. And within a couple of seconds she realised that of course he had to have known all along and might even have contributed to this inequality. The shocking fact was that here was an intelligent young woman who, possibly due to her own gender conditioning, did not want to see her boss as anything other than Mr Nice and Fair. And maybe her boss from his point of view was just that, he did not see anything wrong or discriminatory in underpaying her. Influenced by his own gender conditioning, he was not questioning the pay-policies of their company.

If it was part of a country's or company's structure to have fair remuneration and a balanced gender diversity in leadership positions, then equal pay would not have to be addressed on a case by case basis.

We could take a look at ageism. Throughout my daughter's childhood I entered into her desires to experience whatever society offered her particular age group, which gave me a completely different perspective on being alive. And by gathering information from her and her friends, fellow parents and professional educators, I could make informed decisions on questions which were outside my own experience. Yes, I had once been a child but not in the twenty-first century, with mobile telephones and the internet. If, however, I had isolated myself, maintaining an ageist attitude towards young people: *"She is too young to have any worthwhile opinions concerning her well-being, I have lots of experience and responsibility and will make the best decision"*... I believe my choices as a parent would have been ignorant and maybe even harmful.

In the workplace age discrimination can go either way. People may be seen as too young or too old to do a certain job, have a valid opinion or contribute to a certain process. Many of us can probably come up with examples which challenge ageist assumptions, yet it can be surprisingly difficult to have a boss who is years younger than yourself, or to accept advice from someone who in calendar years has less experience. Similarly, to manage and lead others who are older and more experienced needs skill and sensitivity.

However educated and informed we may be there will always be a difference between studying and knowing facts about something and actually having experienced it. If I need to make a decision from a European's point of view on how to set up business in China, I would probably be wise to gather information from a diverse range of sources, including both Europeans and Chinese who have hands on experience in this area. There are even companies which offer such services. Yet on a structural level why do so many companies and governments shy away from their leadership teams being truly diverse? Surely this would logically lead to the most informed decision-making, and therefore increase the success of their company or country? I suspect that the resistance to embracing this structure is partly to do with the GAP feeling.

The more different someone is from us the more we need to use a full range of communication skills to bridge the initial UNDER-STANDING GAP. If we are the one in the minority we need a range of personal communication skills to break through the stereotypical assumptions of our peers and bosses. If we already hold a majority position of power we need to be prepared to move out of our comfort zone in the area of communication habits.

The very fact that someone is different means we cannot rely on easy 'connection' shortcuts. Whether it is the quick joke, shared references (golf, football, politicians, films) or even different likes and dislikes in, for example, food or music. On top of this, memories that seem relevant and comparable to a current situation can lead our thinking down the wrong path, because the following two tendencies may cause us to overlook or undervalue some important differentiating factors.

1. We become attached to people, places, events and things. These bonds can affect the judgements we form about new situations and the appropriate action to take. For example, if our experience working with a particular person went well and was pleasurable, we will be more likely to overlook key, possibly problematic differences when interviewing a 'similar type' of person for a new job.
2. Research has shown that even well-intentioned professionals, such as doctors and auditors, are unable to prevent self-interest from biasing their judgement.

The implications of the above observations are inescapable. To avoid these traps, we need to involve a diverse selection of people in decision-making. If we want best thinking we should insist on diversity within the collaborative structure of our governing bodies. By counterbalancing these subconscious biases we will leave more room for accurate informed analysis and decision-making. It will also be more likely that the decisions made are in the interest of a larger, more diverse group of people. The higher the percentage of people who are thriving in a country, company or social structure, the more stable it is likely to be. A base of stability and well-being can give space for innovative and creative development.

We can change the laws and instate proportional representation concerning diversity in our governing bodies. But for a new balance of diversity to succeed we need to be able to inspire rather than become alienated and frustrated with each other's differences. Developed personal communication skills which can navigate the inevitable increase in UNDERSTANDING GAPs are central to diversity thriving.

Many of the ideas as well as the **AND-DO-ITs** in this book will facilitate this.

AND-DO-IT

Personal Diversity Re-Think

→ Take a moment to consider how many different and diverse kinds of people you interact with on a weekly basis. Consider the categories of race, gender, age, religion, health, intellect, wealth, nationality...

→ Note if there is a difference between the workplace and your home life.

→ If there is an area where you are generally only interacting with a specific type of person, identify what impact this could have on your knowledge base, thinking and decision-making.

→ Could you and would you like to take one action which could make a shift ?

13 Leading & Following
A Brief Look

This section includes five AND-DO-ITs
  ...off with the old and on with the...

Do you consider yourself a leader, a follower or a varying percentage of both?

Could you make a mental list from your early childhood up until now identifying times when you have taken a position of leadership? By which I mean moments or periods of time when you have been responsible for a situation and made decisions which affected other people. And could you make another list of moments when you have followed someone else's desires, ideas or decisions? You will probably be able to come up with examples for both perspectives.

For a simple and even mundane example, it is interesting to note that during something as repetitive as a daily conversation with another person the leadership will probably change back and forth as the individuals interact with each other. As long as both people are also prepared to give up their will and for a moment follow the thoughts of the other, there will be different instances when each of the two people will be either a leader or a follower.

Which box do others put you in? To be a leader seems to have more status built around it than to be a follower. Countries and companies are run and directed by people who are leaders. Even when decisions are made through groups or committees which are run in a reasonably democratic way, there will probably be people who take more active and passive leadership roles. Within the workplace, employees are assessed for their leadership qualities and this will have a direct effect on how they are promoted up through a company's hierarchical power structure. And in turn it will influence the amount of money they earn. Is the quality: *'talented follower'* ever listed on one's performance review? Yet a performance review may value the identity: *'team-player'*. What qualities do individuals possess which help them to be perceived as potential leadership material? If we take raw ability and intelligence as a given, it has been noted that your height, gender, age and skin colour can play a part. The truism that the tall, middle-aged, white male will have a considerable advantage when competing for a leadership position in a western economy, may ring a bell.

Height

As I grew up, I was always tall for my age. Adults often expected me to be more responsible and capable than my shorter friends. I have noticed in the work context that shorter men have a tendency to push themselves forward more assertively when communicating in a group; this is often called *'Napoleon Syndrome'*. And sometimes taller men will try to make themselves smaller and even quieter so as not to be too dominating: *'Tall Man Syndrome'*. These men are clearly not comfortable with the natural advantage concerning access to power which their height gives them. In many cultures the height difference between women and men plays a dynamic role in the mating game. This can seep into the workplace. How does the un-liberated short male executive feel when directing a taller woman who is holding a junior function? Women can choose to change and play with the height dynamic by wearing flat or high-heeled shoes. The taller a person is as they walk into a space, the harder it is to ignore them. In the film industry the leading male actor will usually be filmed in such a way that he appears tall and hence virile. Tom Cruise is a contemporary example, the camera angle is often shot from below. It can be quite a shock to meet one of these idols in the flesh and see how short they really are.

In some cultures the poorer *'common'* person is described as lowly and in the presence of a superior will be required to bow in an attempt to make themselves shorter than the person holding the position of power. Over the centuries we have created crowns and ornate headdresses for our leaders to make them appear taller than everyone else. Somehow height and being higher than others makes a declaration of power. Logically a castle was positioned high on the hill to have a good view over the land; the ruler lived in the castle. In most of the big corporations I have visited, the executive level where the CEO and board of management will have their offices is situated on the top floor of the building. The logic of the castle has woven its way into these modern day office blocks.

Your physical height may be connected to whether or not others perceive you as having leadership qualities. Research has indicated that tall people have an advantage when competing for certain jobs, especially leadership positions. Funnily enough I have found that it is more about the appearance of height rather than the actual inches you may possess. If someone holds themselves with a long, strong, flexible spine and a general physical ease, inhabiting the space around them, they give a feeling of size and height.

This could be described as having physical presence. We can all develop this quality and therefore in my view the need to be born tall can be taken out of the list of leadership clichés.

Gender

A template which is more complicated to change is the one of gender. For thousands of years we have been used to deferring to the easily identifiable male leadership model for the positions of evident power in the workplace and the political arena. Women have usually had to find more circuitous ways to have influence over others. The exceptions are few and notable. And yet if we take a closer look at the definition of leadership, women take many unrecognised leadership responsibilities on a daily basis. The function of parenting, which affects approximately 85% of the world's population, requires the father some of the time and probably the mother most of the time to be a leader. And yet this does not seem to be credited for much when we assess someone's leadership potential and experience for the workplace.

In many societies, female gender conditioning will encourage more inclusive group participation than the typical male gender conditioning. There will be a tendency for women to promote the group rather than themselves. Men, as well as finding it easier to promote themselves, tend to direct their attention either towards other men or towards the person they perceive as holding the position of power. Of course sexual attraction can also influence who in a group discussion will be included or excluded. I have noticed that if someone finds another sexually attractive they will subconsciously either consistently give them more eye contact or not dare look at them at all!

In meetings and discussions, some people go as far as to consciously or subconsciously take other people's ideas and thoughts as their own, and this can be gender related. Women directors describe how often during company meetings when they propose something in a group discussion they are not heard. And then perhaps fifteen minutes later a male colleague says the same idea, claiming the thought as his own, and the rest of the group (usually male) hears, accepts or discusses it. I do not believe that this *'taking of an idea'* is necessarily conscious and it is certainly not a male conspiracy. It could be because the woman is simply not talking with sufficient volume or perhaps she does not project enough physical authority to be seen or heard.

For women to successfully continue changing the balance of leadership perception they need to develop a wide spectrum of communication skills and behaviour patterns to counterbalance entrenched preconceptions.

Age

It occurs to me that if we could, we should identify someone as old or young by counting not from when they were born but from when they die. After all if I die tomorrow I am now very old, but if I die when I am 100 then at the moment I am just past middle aged.

Age or the appearance of a certain age can inspire or deter people from following you. What you say and how old you appear need to be in harmony or cleverly put in juxtaposition. It has been suggested that it is more effective for an older politician to focus on topics of stability coupled with their leadership experience, as these qualities rhyme with their age. Whereas for a younger (or younger looking) politician it seems more effective to declare: "...*the need for change, with refreshing action embracing new ideas*"... "*off with the old and on with the new.*"

From our early childhood the age we appear to be will often be linked to assessing our ability to handle more responsibility. The older child will be asked to look after the younger ones. Children will often want to appear older than they are as then they are more likely to be given power and autonomy by the adults around them. They will gain more rights to do more things and even be allowed to take part in decision-making. Sometimes the difference of only a few months will give a particular child a more dominant position among their peers.

If you are an ambitious young adult you will want to be taken seriously and be given more credit and power to match your desires. In the business world I often see young men putting on their '*older man*' suit in an attempt to give themselves more authority. The businessman who looks particularly young and boyish for his age may also be drawn to over-use a serious communication persona. The older looking person may over-use humour and chumminess to try to appear younger, as looking '*too old*' can also work against promotion and job opportunity. Women too get caught up in the age confusion: striving to maintain a youthful, slim, wrinkle-free appearance together with ageless authority. In a cross cultural arena an individual's age can be harder to gauge. When I meet businesswomen with years of experience, top class degrees and professorships, from countries such as Japan, China and Thailand, they often talk about how frustrated and insulted they are with being treated as if they are little girls, by their European or North American colleagues.

I am regularly taken aback by the GAP between someone's quoted age and how they appear and behave when I meet them. The variations are intriguing. I find the most inspiring people and leaders are the ones who have the capacity to show and inhabit the many ages of their personality. My mother was a great example of this. For years she was a headmistress of a primary school in London. I saw in both her professional as well as her private life, that she regularly showed a full spectrum of age and authority. She could be formidable and imposing, warm and understanding, humorous and sometimes helplessly laughing like a young girl with a youthful twinkle in her eye right up to the day before she died at the age of eighty-nine.

To be able to show a spectrum of age regardless of your actual years, through your communication behaviour, you need to maintain flexibility with your body and your mind, constantly keeping open to different perspectives. This can be an inspiring and surprisingly useful leadership quality.

And as we know a young child can be very wise and an old person remarkably foolish, so best not to assume.

Ethnicity
The colour of someone's skin coupled with their ethnic background and nationality will have a big effect on their access to power and leadership. It does not only depend on being the majority race in a country or company. This subject is too complex to be given the attention it deserves in this book. Cross cultural leadership and communication is becoming increasingly relevant as more and more companies work a global market. As noted in the previous section: Diversity & Decision-Making, to have an eloquent and varied repertoire of communication skills is vital to not only understand and inspire one another but also to be able to short-circuit often unconscious but deep-rooted prejudices.

It can certainly be useful to understand the basic interaction habits of a culture you do business with. This kind of information is readily available in many travel guides or on the internet. But beyond these basic cultural habits and etiquettes, whatever the cross cultural mix of people I have noticed there are two common themes which can close the UNDERSTANDING GAP.

Firstly the common language being used will not be everyone's mother tongue. Consequently there will be a disparity in the speed at which people can speak and understand. The importance of being able to align this is discussed in Golden Classics, section: Tempo, Timing & Cross Cultural Understanding.

Secondly one over-riding connector is emotion. If you feel a strong emotion, other people who are in the same space as you will most probably empathise and feel it too, whether they want to or not. I have found it does not matter where you have grown up or what your particular cultural conditioning has been: we all have and will repeatedly experience the same core emotions, including fear, joy, pain, empathy, anger and pleasure. If as a leader in a cross cultural context you can engage in well chosen real emotions as you communicate, a fundamental connection will be made. The GAP will reduce and the fact that some of the actual words have not been understood becomes less threatening or irritating. With this more secure personal connection, each person gains the desire and confidence to seek accurate understanding, through, for example, further questions and fewer assumptions. The core emotions and how to have ease and access to them are described in section: What & How Do Others Remember What You Have Said?

The Strongest or Weakest Link?
If you want to lead, people have to be prepared to follow. Clearly if no-one follows you, you cannot lead. Perhaps obvious but it is surprising how often a designated leader, in attempting to inspire and lead

a group of people, may for example simply be talking so fast or quietly that hardly anyone can follow their ideas. As discussed in many sections in this book, during interpersonal communication, individuals may have habits which make it hard and sometimes impossible to follow or interact with their ideas even if they are a brilliant thinker.

Lack of clear leadership can have an effect on group intelligence, making it stronger or weaker than each individual in it. Years ago, together with three friends, I bought a beautiful apartment by the sea in southern Spain. We were all intelligent, capable and used to running our individual freelance careers. But as a group, during the buying procedure we missed crucial legal details which could have been disastrous. All four of us were subconsciously leaning on the supposed ability of the other three, probably not wanting to dominate by taking the lead. In the process the intelligence of the group became lower than that of any one of the individual members.

Sometimes peer group pressure can cause individuals to do something that, by themselves, they would not dare to do. Individuals become led by the group. This can be destructive: an individual provoked by the group might commit acts of violence, take drugs or drink too much alcohol. It can also create positive acts of bravery or generosity. But even within an organic group, with seemingly no designated leader, there will tend to be *'a leader of the pack'*.

It would be easy to list the numerous leaders through history who were or became quite mad and yet large numbers of people kept on willingly following them. The population would even become enthused by the leader's cruel or reckless actions. It has often been suggested that when someone is in a position of unchallenged power it can have an unhinging effect. In 1887 the historian and moralist commonly known as Lord Acton expressed in a letter to Bishop Mandell Creighton the subsequently much quoted phrase: *'Power tends to corrupt and absolute power corrupts absolutely...'*

The well-being of the whole group may not be one of the considerations of a designated leader. Sometimes people who are emotionally unbalanced can have considerable charm and brilliant incidental ideas. This makes it all the more important that we clearly see a spectrum of any proposed leader's qualities and do not get seduced by spectacular moments or actions.

On today's political stage, particularly in some democratic countries where the television debate has become popular during election time, the politicians who have simple, expressive and unfortunately often one-dimensional or extreme points of view successfully appeal to the masses. The more intellectual opponent, with the complex and informed view on the economy, will all too often have fluffy communication skills. This may be because during their education they focussed all their energy on developing their intellect and have undervalued the importance of communicating their message so that it is received and understood by others. The present sound bite culture is hypnotic. Deep down we know as we watch the commercial for a soap powder that the housewife is an actress who is being paid to say the product *"…has changed my life!"* Just like we know if a politician promises us the moon that they will sooner or later break that promise. Some of the power and success of these kinds of statements will be realised by the style and technique, not the content. Now more than ever, communication skills play a pivotal part in the success or failure of an individual's bid for leadership and power.

Ideas and Responsibility
If you are in a leadership position, it is easy to fall into the trap of believing that it is only you, all by yourself, who must come up with the best ideas. Some companies seem to encourage passivity amongst their members, which contributes to entrenching an autocratic model. It can make unnecessary pressures on the leader and not leave much space for the creative capital of company members. In group discussions it is a recurring realisation that: *"one of the roles*

of 'The Leader' is to guide decision-making, not necessarily come up with all the important concepts themselves." Maybe it is hard to remember this with the relentless attempts by mass media to either congratulate or accuse the figureheads of our society for their individual accomplishments or mistakes.

Some leaders are attracted by the illusion of control which makes it hard for them to accept moments of leadership from anyone else in their day-to-day interactions. If they dare to regularly give this up and follow the ebb and flow of their colleagues' contributions it creates relationships where everyone is engaged. If a leader dominates, leaving little room for others to contribute or make decisions, then like a muscle the workforce's decision-making ability atrophies. Those many small moments when someone feels they are permitted to choose and lead an action, for example to do something as minor as opening a window, will impact on their general input into an organisation, group of friends or family unit. We can see this particularly with the development of children. The leadership skill is to know how much space and responsibility to give to the people around you at any given moment. And to know that, even when you give people space, it does not guarantee you will be liked or even appreciated.

A leader needs to be able to listen well, speak clearly with engaged emotion and know when to make a decision and visibly take the lead and when to lead from behind – maybe suspending personal conclusions to give others the space to go through a collaborative thinking process. Leadership is a shared activity.

AND-DO-IT
Re-Finding Your Full Height

→ Stand with your feet wider than normal.

→ Slowly, vertebra by vertebra, curl forwards leading with the weight of your head.

→ Keep your neck loose with a heavy head, arms loose and floppy.

→ As your roll down, slightly bend your knees.

→ Once you are tipped over as far as you can without falling over, take a couple of deep breaths.

→ Slowly, starting from the base of your spine, vertebra by vertebra build up your backbone, until you are once again standing upright.

→ As you are rolling up, have the image of lengthening your spine with a little more space in between each vertebra.

→ Make sure that your end position is with your head balancing easily on the last atlas vertebra with the back of your neck lengthened (rather than your head tipping back slightly, hence shortening the back of your neck).

AND-DO-IT
You Lead – Who Leads

During a conversation with one other person consciously notice when they are taking a leading role.
Notice what you do to take the lead and direct the conversation in another direction.

Do you for example:
→ Bluntly say *"let's talk about something else?"*

→ Bring in an alternative topic?

→ Talk about the same topic with a different volume, speed or emotion?

→ Disagree and propose another point of view?

→ Physically move away to do something small (get a glass of water) and then return?

Play with the above possibilities with both men and women and notice the different dynamics.

AND-DO-IT
Who Decides What?

Think of five significant people in your professional life and five from your family and friends.

Using the following three points, assess the percentage of dominance/leadership in a regular type of interaction with each one of them:

1. The topics discussed.

2. The length and time of a meeting.

3. The choice of location.

   Notice if gender or age has anything to do with the above choices.

AND-DO-IT
Why-Buy-It

Choose an advertisement on television or one of those sales clips which regularly repeats itself, and watch it several times.

→ One time focus on the physicality of the people in it.

→ One time focus on the emotions in the presenter's or actors' voice(s).

→ One time focus on the content of what they are saying.

Notice when you become inspired to buy the product and which communication skills they are using each time.

P.S. *Someone may have inspiring and superb communication skills in your daily life, appearing to be genuine and trustworthy, and yet they are not! I have a financial adviser who has an incredibly warm deep voice. Just the sound of this voice tempts me to follow his advice. I am therefore doubly vigilant with the information he gives me.*

AND-DO-IT
Strategic Delegating

Notice if there is someone you know or work with who has become particularly passive.

If you think it may be due to them not having enough leadership opportunities, give them more responsibility and autonomy in some defined actions.

Be prepared to let go of how you might choose to do a certain thing, if you were to do it yourself.

Notice any changes in their motivation.

About the author

Jessie Gordon was born and grew up in London. After studying Theatre and Performance at Dartington College of Arts, in south-west England, she worked for almost ten years as an actress in avant-garde theatre, most notably with the Pip Simmons Theatre Group, performing throughout Europe. She moved briefly into the world of music, playing the bass guitar in the rock band Flex, before going to live in Amsterdam, the Netherlands, where she has been resident ever since. Overlapping with her work in the performing arts Jessie developed a career as an illustrator/cartoonist for newspapers, magazines, postcard series and books, and also as a visual artist exhibiting in London, Tokyo and various locations in the Netherlands. More than twenty years ago, motivated by her ongoing exploration of the art of communication, Jessie co-created the company Executive Performance Training (EPT) **www.executiveperformancetraining.com** of which she is managing director to this day. Based in Amsterdam, EPT specialises in compact personal development programmes which connect the knowledge and techniques of effective live communication with leadership, diversity and cross cultural collaboration. These programmes take place in Europe, North America, Asia and Russia.

In 2011, prompted by her own hospital experiences with both a broken ankle and a lung embolism, Jessie developed the PAC-CARD (Patient Action Communication Card) and sponsored the creation of **www.pac-card.com**, which offers a 'free-download card' containing a checklist of essential support questions, for patients to use in any interaction with a health worker. This will be published accompanied by a handbook and notebook in spring 2013.

Jessie lives in Amsterdam with her partner and has two children.